JFK, *The* Kennedys *and* Me

(NEVER BEFORE TOLD STORIES ABOUT
JFK AND THE KENNEDY CLAN)

LESTER S. HYMAN

Copyright © 2019 Lester S. Hyman
All rights reserved
First Edition

PAGE PUBLISHING, INC.
New York, NY

First originally published by Page Publishing, Inc. 2019

ISBN 978-1-64424-932-1 (Paperback)
ISBN 978-1-64424-934-5 (Hardcover)
ISBN 978-1-64424-933-8 (Digital)

Printed in the United States of America

Dedication

I dedicate this book to David, Andrew and Elizabeth Hyman who have given me unconditional love and support despite my idiosyncrasies.

John Fitzgerald Kennedy was a very complex person. We knew him, not just as our President, but as a father, son, brother, and husband. However, I venture to say that no one knew him quite as I did...as his mentee.

How improbable that this utterly pragmatic Irish Catholic politician would take me, a young Jewish lad fifteen years his junior under his wing. Was it merely political pragmatism? Or was it one of those unusual events where two people, years apart, but perhaps emotionally in sync, formed a unique bond?

For many years now, I've tried to figure out how it was, and why it was, that a United States Senator who became President of the United States of America began, and continued to have, a close personal and professional relationship with me, a young man then still in his twenties, until the day that he died.

I think that somehow it had to do with the make-up of the huge Kennedy family...a total of eight children.

Although he loved his sisters, JFK's daily interface was with his brothers.

The conventional wisdom Is that JFK idolized his older brother Joe with whom there was a two-year difference in age. Asked if he had a happy childhood, Jack always said "yes", but the truth is that his brother Joe was a bully. Rose Kennedy chronicled that Joe Jr.'s temperament was different from Jack's in many ways...and that, during the early years of their childhood, there were terrible fights between them that she described as real battles. But when Joe Kennedy, at age 29, was shot down in his U.S. Air Force bomber plane while defending his country in World War II, and despite their differences, I don't think that Jack's sorrow ever completely went away.

Robert Kennedy was eight years younger than Jack. They had extremely different temperaments, so the two young men were not at all close in those early years and had little in common. It was much later, as adults, that Bobby, initially at the insistence of their father, Ambassador Joseph P. Kennedy, became the key person in Jack's rising political fortunes. Only then did Jack and Bobby finally learn to rely upon one another.

And then there was Teddy who was only five years old when Jack Kennedy was a young man so they never were close to one another because of their fifteen year age difference.

So, despite the fact that the Kennedys were a huge family (3 boys and 5 girls), Jack, as a young man, never was close emotionally with any of his male siblings.

Then along came me, all of 25 years old, and JFK was 40, when we met, perhaps fulfilling Kennedy's need for a young friend whom he could help and enjoy, something that he did until the end of his life. As for me, as an only child, I was very responsive to someone whom I could look upon like an older brother.

But what of JFK's father, whom his sons loved but some of whose views were despicable? There is no question but that Joseph P. Kennedy, JFK's father, was antisemitic. Ron Kessler, in his biography of Joseph P. Kennedy, wrote that Joe Kennedy made it clear that he thought that the Jews had "brought on themselves" whatever Hitler did to them. Biographer Nigel Hamilton wrote that Joseph P. Kennedy met with President Franklin D. Roosevelt at the White House on October 16, 1944 and insisted that the President "was surrounded by Jews and Communists and urged FDR to sack them all". This bigotry was anathema to JFK.

So, whether conscious or subconscious, JFK perhaps saw in his friendship with me, a Jewish person, a repudiation of his father's antisemitism and, unlike his brother Joe, formed with me a brotherly relationship without any bullying or fighting.

For many years now, I secretly have treasured our unique relationship, and only recently decided to make public some of the stories of my involvement with JFK, many of them in order to demonstrate his wonderful sense of humor.

Although I moved heaven and earth to persuade JFK to be my mentor, once that relationship had been achieved, it was he who initiated our get-togethers by calling me from time to time to arrange the place to meet.

No one else knows now, or knew then, about our unique relationship...not even my own family.

The first part of this book is about my seven years together with JFK from when we first met in 1957 until November of 1963 when he left us.

The second part of the book has stories about my interface with other members of the Kennedy clan (Rose, Bobby, Ted, John Jr., Sarge, and Eunice). I hope you enjoy them. Let me tell you now how our unique friendship came about.

First, though, let me explain how I got into politics and came to know John Fitzgerald Kennedy. As an undergraduate at Brown University (1948-1952) I majored in Political Science and soon decided not just to *read* about politics but also to do something about it. That first "something" was to run for office, to wit: Brown's student government. My campaign slogan was "Get More with Les". Corny, but it worked...I won. Thus my appetite was whetted to learn more about politics in the real world. In my senior year at Brown, I was able to convince a Rhode Island radio station to hire me to go to Chicago and broadcast daily 15-minute radio interviews with both Democratic and Republicans leaders whom I got to meet and learn more about, at their respective national conventions. After graduation from Brown, on to Columbia University Law School where, in addition to my studies, I campaigned on behalf of Averill Harriman and Franklin D. Roosevelt Jr. who later became my law client. In 1955 I graduated from Columbia with a Bachelor of Laws degree and went to Washington as an attorney with the U.S. Securities and Exchange Commission. Being in our nation's capital gave me the opportunity to learn firsthand about the U.S. Senate and House of Representatives. It was then that I watched, and began reading affirmatively about, a young Senator from Massachusetts named John Fitzgerald Kennedy who was beginning to make a favorable national reputation for himself. I was intrigued. JFK was smart, articulate and young, so, in my mind, he became the perfect role model for my going into politics. I then and there made up my mind to get to know him and seek his help in getting me started in politics in his, and soon my, home state of Massachusetts. But that was not as easy as it sounds.

Having read every political biography I could get my hands on, I came to the conclusion that the best way to begin in politics was to have a patron. After examining the field, I chose John F. Kennedy as the "planet" to whom I would hitch my star...if he would have me. By 1957 Senator Kennedy already was considered a national figure. I tried a number of times to arrange an appointment with him but, because I wasn't from his home State of Massachusetts (I was born and educated in Providence, Rhode Island) he wasn't about to meet privately with a young junior attorney at the SEC. Initially, I had no luck. After many attempts, I went to see JFK's long-time Administrative Assistant, Ted Reardon, and explained that, although I originally was from Rhode Island, I now had decided to move to Massachusetts and wanted to get to know Senator Kennedy and seek his help in my getting into politics there. Mr. Reardon finally relented and arranged my very first brief appointment with Senator Kennedy. JFK took time out from his work to ask me some questions: Why did I decide to move from Rhode Island to Massachusetts? What was my educational background? Why did I want to get involved in politics? And why him? It was in that brief time that I thought that something had clicked between us but I wasn't sure. It turned out that, in those few moments, Kennedy, who could be cold and calculating toward political rivals, became extremely supportive and encouraging to this young man who was so interested in public service. He agreed to help me and told me to come see him at his apartment in Boston when I was ready to move to Massachusetts. He then kindly autographed a copy of his "Profiles in Courage" book for me. If, God forbid, fire ever broke out in my home, after my family and the dog, the first thing I would save is my autographed copy of "Profiles in Courage". (NOTE: JFK was only 38 years old when he wrote "Profiles in Courage". If today an historian would write a *contemporary* Profiles in Courage book, in my opinion he would have to include John F. Kennedy whose superb diplomacy convinced Russia's leader, Nikita Khrushchev, at the very last moment, to withdraw all Russian nuclear facilities from Cuba, thus avoiding an almost certain nuclear war between the U.S. and Russia. That, to me, took courage.)

After I had my first brief meeting with JFK, I learned that he told his AA Ted Reardon to keep an address card on me for future reference. As the old popular song goes: Who could ask for anything more?

Thrilled at having successfully climbed the first rung on my ladder toward a career in politics, I returned to my job at the SEC but, shortly thereafter, and to my surprise, I was drafted into the United States Navy and served there for two years. It was one of the most formative experiences of my life. I learned that, despite the varied racial and economic backgrounds of my fellow sailors, people are pretty much alike in the sense that the immutable laws of human nature unite us all. It was a great learning experience.

After "boot camp" in Bainbridge, Maryland, I went to sea aboard a U.S. Destroyer Escort named the USS Calcaterra DER 390. My rank was as low as anyone can get in the Navy...I was a Seaman. We went round and round in the middle of the

Pacific Ocean on what they called "picket" duty. The ship did not have any officers with law degrees aboard, but, according to the Navy's rules and regulations, it was necessary to have someone act as the Legal Officer. So the Captain decided that, despite my lowly rank, I, as a Columbia University Law School graduate with an LLB Degree, and a member of the Bar of both the Commonwealth of Massachusetts and the United States Supreme Court, henceforth would serve as the ship's "Legal Officer" which I happily did.

I now was on Senator Kennedy's mailing list (Ted Reardon regularly mailed me copies of Senator Kennedy's speeches in envelopes on the front of which were stamped the "frank" of United States Senator John F. Kennedy...no stamps needed). One day the Captain called me into his cabin. "Hyman", he said, "I see that you've received a letter from Senator John F. Kennedy. "Yessir", I said. "How is the Senator?" asked the Captain. "Just fine", said I. "Did he ask you anything about this ship...or her Captain?" Obviously, the Captain thought - wrongly - that I was some kind of a spy for Senator Kennedy examining his conduct as Captain of the Calcaterra. At that moment, an outrageous idea came to mind. "I'm terribly sorry, Captain," said I mischievously, "but I cannot discuss the contents of Senator Kennedy's letters to me" (which usually were no more than copies of JFK's most recent speeches)... but the Captain didn't know that, and I wasn't about to let on. From that moment on, I was treated like a prince aboard that ship! Later, when I was given a four day leave, I persuaded two of my ship buddies to help drive me from Florida (where the ship was temporarily docked) back to Massachusetts where I attended a meeting that was addressed by Jack Kennedy. When it was over, I had a chance to talk briefly with the Senator. I told him the story of the Captain and the franked letter...he loved it.

In 1957 JFK already was aiming at the presidency of the United States. But first he had to become the nominee of the Democratic Party. For that very reason, the spotlight always was on him as a putative President. But there were other Democratic leaders ready to run for President in 1960, the most prominent of whom was Lyndon Baines Johnson who was the powerful Senate Majority leader. It was the Southerner against the New Englander. I tell you this because, while I was aboard the USS Calcaterra in the Navy, I received a fascinating letter from JFK that I set forth here for your interest.

JOHN F. KENNEDY
MASSACHUSETTS

COMMITTEES:
LABOR AND PUBLIC WELFARE
GOVERNMENT OPERATIONS
SELECT COMMITTEE ON
SMALL BUSINESS

United States Senate
WASHINGTON, D. C.

August 7, 1957

Dear Lester:

I am most grateful for your interest in the Civil Rights legislation and your thoughtfulness in conveying your views on it to me.

I thoroughly share your interest in the passage of legislation which will provide effective safeguards for essential civil rights -- especially voting rights. The passage of such legislation was uppermost in my mind during the entire debate. As the discussion in the Senate was extended and complex, I have endeavored to set down my thinking on its various elements. Because I believe that you are entitled to a full exposition of my position, I am attaching a memorandum elaborating my views. Also, since I feel that they represent a fair and objective appraisal of a critical aspect of the debate, I am enclosing copies of recent editorials from the Washington Post, which has always advocated strong civil rights legislation, and the Washington Evening Star.

I know you appreciate that in the final analysis decisions of legislators must be based on the most careful assessment of all elements under consideration -- in short, votes on specific issues are largely matters of judgment. I trust that after reading the attached memorandum you will discern that my decisions were taken in the interest of the enactment of effective civil rights legislation.

With every good wish.

Sincerely yours,

John F. Kennedy

JFK:ps
Enclosures

Mr. Lester S. Hyman
U.S.S. Calcaterra
Care of Fleet Post Office
New York, New York

DETAILED STATEMENT OF SENATOR JOHN F. KENNEDY ON CIVIL RIGHTS LEGISLATION

My position on the issue of preserving and strengthening the rights of all citizens is a matter of public record. Since I have been in Congress I have unceasingly supported legislation extending and enlarging civil rights. I have repeatedly made efforts to amend Rule XXII to provide for a reasonable limitation on debate -- a position, I regret to say, which has not been shared in the past by many of my colleagues who have rather recently become civil rights advocates.

Although I did not agree with the unusual procedure of placing the bill before the Senate without prior consideration by committee because of the dangerous precedent this set, I did firmly indicate my commitment to an early discharge of the bill from the Judiciary Committee. I shared the view of those who voted to place the bill directly on the calendar that the bill must be considered before the adjournment of this session of Congress. I voted to call the bill from the calendar and resisted efforts to return the bill to committee. My vote was cast against the deletion of Title III, which provided additional and substantial guarantees of existing civil rights. I am still concerned by the efforts of some States to prevent victims of intolerance from seeking representation by private agencies and public authority. Such forms of interposition might effectively have been barred under Title III.

On the controversial Title IV of the bill, I voted with such outstanding and longstanding friends of civil rights as Senators Anderson, Pastore and Jackson. With respect to the point at issue -- whether jury trials should be required in criminal contempt cases -- it was a rather generally-held opinion among Senators who have had long experience in the law, such as Senators O'Mahoney and Pastore, that it was important to give adequate legal protection to citizens involved in such proceedings. Because of the preeminent necessity to preserve the human and constitutional rights of Negroes who are principally involved, this argument in itself would not have been controlling. However, there is almost universal agreement, even among opponents of the jury trial amendment, that the primary protection of voting rights will take place under the civil power of the courts. For example, a judge under civil proceedings can imprison a voting registrar who refuses to register a Negro voter until he complies with the order of the court. Regardless of intervening time or the commission of other acts, criminal or otherwise, the original action does not lose its civil nature and a jury trial is not required. Consequently, without resort to criminal contempt proceedings, the desired effects can be obtained. Moreover, after the sponsors of the amendment accepted the addition of Senator Church, I felt that the jury trial amendment would also enlarge the opportunities for jury service by Negro citizens who had heretofore been systematically excluded -- an important, though not final, breach of another discrimination.

Although confident that this was a reasonable assessment of the situation, I consulted further with lawyers noted not only for their knowledge of the law but for their dedication to the preservation of civil liberties. One of them, Professor Mark DeW. Howe of the Harvard Law School, wrote --

> "...It is quite clear, I believe, that support of those amendments would not, in all the circumstances, involve a surrender of principle to expediency. I am hopeful, therefore, that if it seems to you that the enactment of Title IV will be jeopardized without the O'Mahoney amendment, you will support that amendment.
>
> "May I thank you for giving me this opportunity for expressing my views. I need not add that I was delighted by the position which you took on Title III - a position which does you great credit."

Another, Professor Paul Freund, said --

> "...The upshot is that there would be some sacrifice of effectiveness in limiting the power of the judge alone to cases of civil contempt. Against this loss must be weighed the value of a more receptive sentiment on the part of the original opponents of the bill, a sentiment which presumably would filter down to the press and populace of the South. In the long run that state of mind may be more important than the partial sacrifice of legal procedures involved in the compromise. This is a matter of judgment on which your own wisdom will yield a better answer than any I might venture. I can only say that to accept the jury trial for criminal contempt would not in my view constitute a betrayal of principle."

Several other lawyers of high repute confirmed this view of the merit and validity of the O'Mahoney amendment.

The second consideration which led me to accept the O'Mahoney amendment was a practical one. My observation of the debate led me to believe that the bill would have been filibustered if a jury trial amendment had not been adopted and that it would have been impossible to obtain cloture. In addition to the very real danger of prolonging debate on this important legislation indefinitely and in the end perhaps losing it, there is the important fact that opponents of the measure would have been able, week after week, to broadcast their message that it was they who were fighting for civil rights in their efforts to preserve a jury trial in criminal contempt proceedings. It seemed to me that this would have placed friends of civil rights in an extremely difficult psychological position which was fraught with the most serious implications with respect to maintaining a broad base of support for a strong civil rights bill.

As you know, there has not been an effective civil rights bill passed by Congress since Reconstruction days. This year, for the first time, such an opportunity has presented itself. I consider it especially vital to assure enactment of such a law at this session of Congress -- especially since it concerns voting rights, whose implementation will make it much easier to secure for all citizens their other civil rights. The bill contains a provision establishing a commission which has extensive powers and which, if properly directed, can pave the way for future extensions of civil rights. Title III, which granted strong civil powers to the Attorney General in connection with rights other than voting rights, unfortunately was eliminated. I voted for the retention of this important section and regret that it did not carry. It would be a heavy blow to free government to exchange a bill of real merit for the doubtful satisfaction of standing dogmatically by a provision which does not preserve a genuine principle or add significantly to the substantive effect of the measure.

An aspect of this debate which has generally been overlooked is that there is now consensus on a reasonable and effective civil rights program. Those who would block its enactment by spurious arguments do no service to the cause of civil rights. Enactment of this bill marks the end of an era during which it has been impossible to get effective legislation to insure the protection of basic human and civil rights. Therefore, action on legislation now is as important in terms of future protections of civil rights as it is for the substantial immediate effect which it will have.

I've never seen it published anywhere else. It was about civil rights and, in particular, voting rights, which was an extremely sensitive issue both in the North and in the South. The Northern liberals were for assuring minorities (namely black people) the right to vote while most of the very conservative Southerners were against it. Like you, I found the letter and its attachments very difficult to fathom. In essence, though, Kennedy wanted to follow the proper procedures for guaranteeing voting rights for minorities by first holding Congressional hearings. But his putative opponents (LBJ in particular), as well as then Vice President Nixon, wanted to skip the hearings and go directly to the vote. They tried to convince people that Kennedy thus was trying to stall the voting rights bill when, in truth, JFK was a fierce supporter of minority rights but wanted to do it the right way. To skip the hearings, he said, would set a dangerous precedent. Kennedy then turned to two distinguished law professors who argued that the Senate should follow proper procedures to achieve their goal and thus agreed with JFK's position. Kennedy won (the proper procedures were followed) but his opponents (LBJ et al) said it was only *they* who were the friends of minorities.

I realize that the foregoing documents are rather complicated and often quite difficult for the layman to follow and comprehend. But basically what they explain is how the U.S. Senate strengthened the effectiveness of civil rights legislation by establishing new safeguards against the exclusion of Negroes from jury service in Federal courts. Senator Kennedy played an important role in achieving that excellent result. In doing so, however, he was constantly under attack by white Southern leaders for being too liberal in his demands, while, at the same time, he was being criticized by many black leaders who felt that he did not go far enough in meeting their demands. But Kennedy's concerns throughout was to come up with language that actually could pass the Congress and be signed by the President, which indeed it was. He persevered in helping to shape a final bill that effectively made it easier for Negroes to participate in the judicial process, thus helping the black community achieve its goals. By so doing, JFK acted in the national interest rather than becoming captive to either of the warring factions (the whites in the south or the blacks in the north). As a footnote, it is interesting to note that in 1979 (in the case of Duren v. Missouri) Ruth Bader Ginsburg argued before the Supreme Court basically the same issue as above but that *women* also should be granted the right to sit on a jury.

My old friend Ted Sorensen, former Special Counsel to JFK, wrote in his biography of Kennedy, that "in more than one speech JFK would quote, with understanding as well as amusement, a legendary verse said to have been found among the papers of a deceased legislator:

Among life's dying embers
These are my regrets:
When I'm "right" no one remembers,
When I'm "wrong" no one forgets

When I received my Honorable Discharge from the Navy, I headed home to Providence, Rhode Island, tossed my Navy hat onto the roof of my house and moved to Massachusetts where I was to live for the next twelve years. The year was 1957 - I was 26 years old – and I opened up my own solo law office. Soon I learned that Senator Kennedy was going to speak before an open audience in the town of Brookline...I do not remember the exact date...so of course I went there to hear him. After JFK's speech and the Q. and A. session was over (to great applause), he noticed me and gestured for me to come up on the stage. Was I ever impressed! There were a few quick pleasantries and he then said he was looking forward to our get-together at his Bowdoin Street apartment. While I was talking with the Senator, I noticed that a photographer had taken some photos, so I asked him if he would take one of the two of us (JFK and I) together, and would he give me a copy. He said "yes" and did – that photo is set forth here in my book. Soon it was time to take the plunge into politics, so, taking JFK at his word, I arranged for an appointment with him as he had suggested, to seek his advice.

We met at the Kennedy apartment at 122 Bowdoin Street in Boston which is right across the street from the State Capitol - it's next door to the Bellevue Hotel (known affectionately as the Bell-a-view) where all the pols hung out after work. I remember once asking Maurice "Mossy" Donahue, the then President of the Massachusetts Senate, whether it was necessary for me to go drinking there if I was going to become involved in Massachusetts politics. "Only if you want to become an alcoholic", he advised.

The apartment at 122 Bowdoin was the political home of the Kennedy family - it was their voting residence and here was where they did their political business (as distinguished from Hyannisport in Cape Cod which was the Kennedy family residence).

You would knock on the door of the apartment which was quite small and more than modest - it would open a crack and an "old faithful" Kennedy retainer, Francis X. Morrissey, would peep out and consult his list to see whether you should be admitted. Fortunately I was on the list.

After sitting in the reception area for a few minutes, I was ushered into the presence of "Himself' as the Irish like to say. Even as I write this - at the age of 87 - I remember clearly the charisma that emanated from JFK. Unlike good manners, charisma cannot be learned - you either have it or you don't and Kennedy had it...in spades.

He was casually, but immaculately, dressed (khaki pants and a sport shirt). One leg was draped over his desk chair, and he was continuously taking phone calls with one hand on the phone receiver while, in the other hand, he held a pencil that he kept tapping away at the desk. At this particular moment he was talking with Tom Winship, the Editor of the Boston Globe, trying to persuade Tom not to run a story that JFK was seen driving with Frank Sinatra on the highway to Cape Cod. Sinatra was well known as a swinger and this was not the image that Kennedy wanted to portray to the mostly conservative voters of Massachusetts.

The pencil was a left-over from Kennedy's initial nervousness in speaking in public. At that time, his hands constantly fidgeted, so someone suggested that he hold a pencil in both hands to quiet them down - it worked so well that, even when he wasn't actually holding a pencil while he spoke, his hands would look as if they were.

The Senator had a deep tan - only later did we learn that the tan was a conscious effort to conceal a yellowish pallor that marked someone who suffered from Addison's disease, a serious kidney ailment that never became known to the public until after his death.

His hair was auburn colored and, with the sunshine coming in through the window, it took on a reddish hue that rarely showed up in photographs. To me, he was golden.

After a few preliminary remarks, I came to the point. I told him I wanted to become active in Massachusetts politics and asked whether I could work for him in his 1958 re-election campaign

He laughed. "That would be too easy," he said. "I've already made it...so you've got to do what I did...learn politics from the ground up." I was more than willing.

He then suggested that I start at the city level by working for an old friend of his, Edward F. McLaughlin Jr. who was running for re-election to the Boston City Council. He told me that he would write a letter to Eddie and tell him to expect a call from me with his (JFK's) blessing.

Then he promised to keep track of my progress and see me from time to time to report. I was in seventh heaven as I left his presence feeling that I had come in contact with a rocket to the moon, a superhuman being touched with greatness who would go all the way.

I should add that these impressions were formed *before* JFK became President or even was talked about as a serious presidential candidate. Oftentimes people come away from a meeting with a President of the United States raving about that person's charismatic qualities. I submit, however, that much of that feeling is attributable to the aura that the *office,* not the person, emanates. After all, the President of the United States arguably is the most powerful human being in the world, so how could one not help but be overwhelmed in the presence of such a person? But Kennedy brought his own aura to the table long before he became President which later became magnified and enhanced *after* he became President.

As he promised, JFK wrote to an old friend of his, Edward F. McLaughlin Jr. who was running for re election to the Boston City Council (which he won) and asked him to take me under his wing and teach me about the basics of political campaigning. Eddie immediately responded in the affirmative, we met, and I was put to work (gratis, of course).

```
JOHN F. KENNEDY                                           COMMITTEES:
  MASSACHUSETTS                                        FOREIGN RELATIONS
                                                    LABOR AND PUBLIC WELFARE

                         United States Senate
                             WASHINGTON, D. C.

                              July 31, 1957


      Lester S. Hyman
      U.S.S. Calcaterra (Der-390)
      Care of Fleet Post Office
      New York, New York


      Dear Lester:

             Many thanks for your letter of recent date.

             I have been very glad to write to Eddie McLaughlin
      in your behalf and telling him that you will be in Boston
      between August 11th and 15th on leave. I would suggest
      that you call him at the City Hall upon your arrival in
      Boston and I am sure that he will be very glad to see
      you.

             With every good wish.

                                       Sincerely yours,

                                       John F. Kennedy

      JFK:el
```

Eddie began by showing me how to hand out campaign literature. When you slip political flyers under apartment doors at night, you learn a lot about dogs! A non sequitur? Not at all. Dogs usually don't take to strangers shoving pieces of paper under the doors of the apartment or home where they live. I was barked at, charged at, bitten and drooled upon. But overall Kennedy was right - if you finally get in the door and talk to the voters, it's the best way to learn what motivates them, find out what issues they really care about, tell them what you would do about them, and convince them to vote for you. On the other hand, I'm willing to bet that JFK never went door to door personally handing out campaign literature.

After the 1957 campaign for Boston City Council I felt that I had paid my dues and was ready to move up to the next plateau: the development of issues.

Eddie McLaughlin next decided to run for Congress in 1958 but was defeated in the Democratic primary by John Saltonstall (yes, a Democratic Saltonstall), so, being a good sport, I went to work for Jock, as he was better known…and did research on issues for him as I always had wanted. One day he asked me to accompany him to a local television studio where he was to tape a political commercial with Senator John F. Kennedy. Jock confided in me that he was nervous because he never before had appeared on TV.

The studio was set up for a rehearsal run-through. Jock sat at his place on the set waiting for Jack Kennedy to appear. He waited. And he waited. Finally he asked me to go see what happened to JFK. I found the Senator relaxing in his dressing room. I showed him the script that I had written for the two of them at Jock's request and asked him to come downstairs for a rehearsal. JFK informed me that he had no need for a script…he knew what he wanted to say…and he didn't like rehearsals because they robbed the final "take" of spontaneity…and that he would come down to the studio when they were ready to shoot.

So I went back to Jock and relayed the bad news. He was upset but decided that I should sit in at the rehearsal and pretend that I was Kennedy so he could get the feel of it. Being a ham at heart, I proceeded to speak in that unique Kennedy cadence: "Jock, I'm pleeshed to be he-ya on your behalf, and I urge the citizens of Massachusetts to vote for you for Congress this yee-ah."

There was a hush in the studio - the camera and technical crew said nothing - I assumed that they were carried away by my eloquent impersonation. Instead I felt a tap on my shoulder, turned around, and found myself face to face with the real John F. Kennedy who quietly had come in the back way. With an amused smile on his face, he said: "Pretty good imitation, Lesh". I was mortified. The camera crew loved it. JFK then slipped into my rapidly vacated chair and recorded his endorsement of Saltonstall in one smooth "take". P.S. In spite of JFK's support, Jock lost. However something productive came out of the experience because I met my future wife, Helen Sidman, who was a Saltonstall assistant.

Thereafter JFK suggested other candidates for whom I would work in order to learn more about political campaigns, including a candidate for Mayor of Boston.

Some months before JFK announced his candidacy for President of the United States, he called me at home one evening and asked whether I would do him a favor. "Of course," I replied without even knowing what he had in mind: "Anything". "I understand that you know Eleanor Roosevelt", said Kennedy. "That's correct", I said (read more on how I came to know this great lady on a separate page). "Leshtah" (that's how JFK pronounced my name with that unique Kennedy accent.) "Next time you see her, I want you to ask Mrs. Roosevelt what she thinks of me for President." "But Senator," I replied, "I really don't know her that well to ask such a sensitive question."

"That's just the point", said Kennedy, "she won't know anything about our relationship so perhaps she'll tell you the truth about her views toward me." "Okay", I said, "I'll try.

So I wrote to Mrs. Roosevelt, and on September 15, 1958 she replied as follows: "Dear Mr. Hyman: Thank you for your letter of the 9th. I could see you at the above address on December 2nd at 3:00pm if that is convenient for you. My apartment number is 1947 and the most convenient bank of elevators is on the 55th Street side. Very sincerely yours, Eleanor Roosevelt."

MRS. FRANKLIN D. ROOSEVELT
202 FIFTY-SIXTH STREET WEST
NEW YORK 19, N. Y.

December 15, 1958

Dear Mr. Hyman:

Thank you for your letter of the 9th.

I could see you at the above address on December 22nd at 3:00 p.m. if that is convenient for you.

My apartment number is 1947 and the most convenient bank of elevators is on the 55th Street side.

Very sincerely yours,

Eleanor Roosevelt

I remember that, when you got there, you sat in a reception room of her lovely apartment before Mrs. R comes to greet you. Soon it was my turn and I was ushered into the living room for my meeting with Mrs. Roosevelt. We chatted for a few moments about current events, especially politics, and finally I got up the courage to ask her the sixty-four dollar question, to wit: "Mrs. Roosevelt, what do you think of Jack Kennedy for President?" Immediately, and to my amazement, she responded: "Oh, Mr. Hyman, we wouldn't want the Pope in the White House, would we?" I thought I'd go into shock. Here was one of the most liberal people in the country telling me what I considered to be a bigoted response about the presidency of the United States. Upon reflection, I knew that Mrs. Roosevelt had been brought up as a child in a very sheltered environment and rarely had interaction with Catholics or Jews or Blacks, and I'm afraid that some of that stuck…nevertheless I was truly shocked by her response to my question.

As soon as I got back to Boston, I called Senator Kennedy and told him, word for word, what Mrs. Roosevelt had said. "That's just what I thought," said Kennedy, and he thanked me very much, thus proving in his mind why Mrs. Roosevelt was so opposed to him for President. Instead Mrs. R supported, and voted for, Adlai Stevenson for the Democratic nomination. Yet, once he became President, JFK generously (and wisely) appointed Mrs. Roosevelt to become America's first Ambassador to the United Nations, a position which she fulfilled with great distinction.

How I Got to Know Eleanor Roosevelt

In 1949, while I was in my Freshman year at Brown University, I helped found Students for Democratic Action (SDA) which was an offshoot of the ADA. As a liberal Democratic organization, we often invited guest speakers to come talk with us about current issues in the country. We had no more than 15 or 20 members and we met monthly.

One day I learned that Eleanor Roosevelt was going to be in Providence, Rhode Island to address the World Affairs Council. I was able to find a mailing address for her and wrote to ask whether, since she was going to be in Providence, Rhode Island (where Brown U. is located), would she be willing to address our SDA campus organization? To my shock and delight, she accepted.

When the University authorities learned that the great lady herself was coming to Brown, they called me into the office of the distinguished President of Brown University (Dr. Henry Merritt Wriston) who told me that it was absurd for me to bring probably the most famous woman in the world to talk to a student group of only 15 members. Instead, he suggested...nay, ordered...that it was such an important event that we should open it up to the entire campus community. I agreed.

On the appointed day, some 1200 students and faculty packed Sayles Hall, our largest campus venue. They literally were hanging from the rafters. I assumed that President Wriston would introduce the former First Lady. Instead he informed me at the last minute that I, a mere Freshman, was to introduce Mrs. Roosevelt. His rationale was that, since I had the audacity to invite the woman, the least I could do was introduce her to the assembled throng. "But," I told Dr. Wriston, "I'm only 18 years old and I've never before spoken in public." "Well, now's your chance", said the University President.

So I practiced and practiced my introduction but, up until the last moment, I couldn't remember whether to address Mrs. R as "Mrs. Franklin Delano Roosevelt" or "Eleanor Roosevelt". When my moment came, I approached the microphone and said: "And now, ladies and gentlemen, it is my honor to present to you the former First Lady of the land...and now First Lady of the world, Mrs. Franklin Delano Eleanor Roosevelt." Everyone started to laugh. I was mortified by this unintentional gaffe of etiquette.

As Mrs. R approached the microphone, the audience roared its greeting. She was a very tall woman. She put her arms around my shoulders, leaned into the microphone and said soothingly: "Oh, Mr. Hyman, that was perfect!" My faux pas marked the beginning of a long and delightful relationship with Eleanor Roosevelt.

Now back to our story.

My friend and mentor Eddie McLaughlin once told me that, if ever I was going to run for office, I should meet Richard Cardinal Cushing, prince of the Boston Catholic Church, he of the craggy face and gravelly voice. Those in the know considered Cushing to have been the real mayor of Boston. He also was very close to the entire Kennedy family, especially Jack Kennedy, so it made sense for me to try and meet this distinguished prelate. I asked Eddie how I could get to know the Cardinal. "Call the Chancery and ask for an appointment", he said. So I screwed up my courage and made the call, fully expecting some lovely nun out of "The Sound of Music" to answer. Instead, a rough voice barked out: "Yass"...it completely threw me off. "I'm calling to request an appointment with Cardinal Cushing" I said. "Who is this?" the voice roared back at me. "My name is Lester Hyman and Eddie McLaughlin suggested that I come to see the Cardinal." I replied, "and who is this?" I asked. "This is the Cardinal", he answered to my shock and surprise. I was absolutely astounded that the man answered his own telephone. We chatted for a few moments and he then granted me an appointment.

On the designated day, I presented myself at the Chancery and was ushered (this time by a nice "Sound of Music" nun who was there after all) into Cushing's office. Again I was taken aback. There he stood in full regalia...with the red hat, the long gown and the big ring. With a wide smile, a crushing handshake, and a reassuring pat on the back, he said: "Siddown, kid". I did.

"Whaddya want?" he asked. "I'm thinking of running for State representative in Ward five", I said, "and I wanted your advice." Whyn't you say so? I love politics", he said, so I told him a little about myself and my hopes for the campaign.

"Ya know what my biggest problem is in Boston?" he asked. "No, sir". "Puerto Ricans", he said. "They're pouring into the city from San Joo-Anne (which I finally figured out was San Juan). "Now I have to get me some Spanish-speaking priests, and they're hard to find." It took me quite a while before I figured out that his mauling of the English language was an act...it was the way His Eminence made himself one of the people. The man-in-the-street adored him. The elite—particularly the Catholic elite (which politicians used to refer to as the "three toilet Irish") were ashamed of him because they felt he was somewhat of a boor. Nothing could be farther from the truth. Cardinal Cushing was an extremely bright and sophisticated man. He spoke Latin fluently. He put on this "front" as an effective way of communicating with the masses. We then had an extremely sophisticated discussion about Massachusetts politics. A week later I received in the mail an enormous photograph of His Eminence in full regalia with the inscription: "To my friend and benefactor, Lester S. Hyman with affection, blessings and gratitude. Richard Cardinal Cushing. Easter 1960."

Of course I couldn't resist telling Eddie McLaughlin about my terrific meeting with the Cardinal, but when I showed him the autographed picture, I thought he'd have a fit. "I'm a good Catholic and the Cardinal won't give me one of those things", he said. He was jealous and I felt bad about it. So later when I again saw the Cardinal, I told him that Eddie McLaughlin was very upset that he didn't have an autographed picture of the Cardinal...and what should I tell him? Cushing gave me a big grin and said: "You just tell Eddie McLaughlin that the Cardinal likes Jews!".

The world remembers watching Richard Cardinal Cushing when he offered the blessings when John F. Kennedy was inaugurated as President...and years later when he presided at JFK's funeral. He was very close to the entire Kennedy family.

The *real* Cardinal Cushing is shown at his best when he was interviewed for the oral history of the John F Kennedy Library. Let me give you a sample of what the Cardinal said:

"From his deep familiarity with history, John Kennedy knew his country and its past better than most presidents. From his own experience in war, he knew the meaning of the phrase "live for country." From his own life in this century, he knew the nature of the dangers that faced his country. He deftly blended these areas of knowledge together to forge a guide for his actions. He loved America and its people. Seeing it as he did in the prime of its prosperity and power, he determined that he must do all that he could to preserve this image for its children and his. He had to reduce the threat of nuclear holocaust without resort to all out war. This was *his* crisis as the first government under the Constitution had been Washington's [George Washington]; the Civil War, Lincoln's [Abraham Lincoln]; the depression, Roosevelt's [Franklin D. Roosevelt]. He knew from history that these men had met their problems with new ideas that drew criticism from friend and foe alike. He knew that contemporary popularity often evaded the innovator. Yet, he went ahead and proclaimed to the world, "Let us never negotiate out of fear. But let us never fear to negotiate." Out of this proclamation came the Nuclear Test Ban Treaty, the "hot line" to Russia, the Peace Corps, and other such innovations. Some groups in America cried, "Soft on Communism!" to his efforts, for they could not fathom as he did that the American system was sufficiently flexible to utilize the many ways and means to preserve peace without risking weakness or sacrificing honor." (The above are quotes from the JFK oral history and demonstrate the real Cardinal Cushing).

* * *

In 1959 JFK is running all out for the presidency of the United States. Having served my political apprenticeship in 1957 and 1958. I decided to use the limited political knowledge I had learned thus far to try my own wings and run for Massachusetts State Representative. Since we lived on the bottom of Beacon Hill, I decided that here was where I should run. Wrong! Ward 5 always had been, and probably always will be, the most Republican district in all of Massachusetts. Before I even could get to the final, however, I had to survive the Democratic primary where five Irishmen also sought the nomination.

Happily, with hard work and more than a little luck, I achieved that goal and came in first. On September 24, 1960, to my surprise and delight, I received the following letter from Senator Kennedy at the very time that he was running for the Presidency of the United States.

U. S. SENATOR...　　**JOHN F. KENNEDY**
　　　　　　　　　　　FOR PRESIDENT
　　　　　　　　　　　★　　★　　★　　★

HEADQUARTERS · 1106 CONNECTICUT AVE., N.W. · WASHINGTON, D. C. · DISTRICT 7-1717

September 24, 1960

Mr. Lester S. Hyman
185 Devonshire Street
Boston 10, Massachusetts

Dear Lester:

    Congratulations upon your nomination as the Democratic nominee for State Representative from Boston's Ward 5. I wholeheartedly endorse your candidacy.

    The state legislature of our Commonwealth faces difficult tasks in the next decade, and we will need legislators with your idealism, your determination and your enthusiasm to meet the problems ahead.

    I urge the voters in Ward 5 to support you in your race for this important office.

    With every good wish, I am

                      Sincerely,

                        John F. Kennedy

JFK:lbf

JFK tried to help me and my campaign in every way possible. One day I received a telephone call at our campaign headquarters from a woman who identified herself as Shelley Winters. The only Shelley Winters I knew of was one of the most famous movie stars in the country at that time. She told me that she was *the* Shelley Winters, that she was in

Boston to publicize her latest movie, and that Jack Kennedy had told her to call me and see whether there was anything she could do to help my campaign. I was flattered. We met in the cocktail lounge of the Ritz-Carlton Hotel, talked about the campaign for a while, and then posed together for a photograph which we placed in the local newspapers. Next I received a campaign contribution ($100) from the popular national late night TV comedian Steve Allen…again, he said that Jack Kennedy told him to help me.

JFK *kept* trying to help me. On September 3rd I got a call from his Senate office telling me that he would be walking from the Boston Ritz-Carlton Hotel where he was staying (remember that I told you earlier that, to my knowledge, he never spent a night at his little apartment at 122 Bowdoin Street…the Ritz was more his style when he was in Boston) to the auditorium where he was going to give a speech and wanted me to know that I could walk with him and his entourage in an effort to give me a last minute publicity boost for my campaign for Ward 5 State Representative. The photo (see attached) appeared in the Boston newspapers but alas, it said only that JFK was "surrounded by Secret Service agents". I guess I looked like one of them and not like a candidate for State Representative.

On election day I lost, but I did better than any Democrat ever had in the history of Ward 5 and received more votes there than most of the Democrats who were running Statewide...but it just was not good enough. It was, however, a great learning experience. Lesson: Don't run just because you're a good man or woman...run in a District where you have a pragmatic chance of winning!

It was during that same walk that JFK presented me with one of his PT 109 tie clips (which shows the Navy ship on which JFK served as an officer during World War II that was bombed by the Japanese, and where he singlehandedly saved the lives of his fellow crew members) which he gave only to close friends and people who occupied key roles in his campaign for the Presidency. I proudly wear it to this day, and every day, as a remembrance of this man who was my great friend and mentor.

My next foray into Massachusetts politics was much more successful. A man named Endicott "Chub" Peabody asked me over and over again, even at my young age, to become his campaign manager in order to help him become Governor of Massachusetts. The odds of Chub even becoming the Democratic *nominee* for Governor were slim, especially since 1) it seemed impossible for a Yankee Protestant to obtain the Democratic nomination for Governor of Massachusetts at a time when most of the delegates to the State nominating convention were Irish-American and Italian-Americans and 2) even if one got the nomination, a popular Italian-American Republican sitting Governor named John Volpe was sure to win re-election to a second term. However I agreed to accept the position as campaign manager. JFK was not at all enthusiastic about my decision to head up Peabody's campaign but made no effort to dissuade me from assuming that position. Together with Joe Koufman who was Chub's law partner and friend, we came up with a unique strategy, to wit: Knowing that most of the Irish and Italian Democratic delegates to the convention had no love for a Yankee named Endicott "Chub" Peabody, we had some of our minions convince the Delegates that this was their chance once and for all to get rid of Peabody. Vote for Chub, they said, give him the nomination, and let him be defeated by Governor Volpe in the finals so he never again would become a factor in Massachusetts Democratic politics. They did just that, and Chub got the nomination. Instead of losing in the final, however, to everyone's surprise, Peabody, won the Democratic nomination for Governor and then, against all odds, won the election itself, defeating the Republican John Volpe in a squeaker (by 4,431 votes out of 4 million cast). Chub became Governor and he appointed me as The Assistant to the Governor. Incidentally, when I, as a very young man, was racing back and forth during the campaign with a grim look of determination on my face, Chub told me to Walk Slowly and Smile which has become a watchword for my life.

In my opinion, Peabody was a good Governor. During his Administration, he proposed and won voter approval for a State constitutional amendment extending the terms of office for all constitutional officers, including the Governor, from two to four years. He advocated laws to prevent discrimination in housing, established drug addiction treatment programs, and strongly opposed capital punishment.

Yet there is no question in my mind that there was a tension...much undeserved...between President John Fitzgerald Kennedy (Irish Catholic) and Endicott Peabody (Yankee Protestant). Soon you will understand why, magnanimously, Chub sent me, a mere 32-year-old, to do the business of Massachusetts in Washington because I was close to President Kennedy and was neither Irish nor Yankee.

To what do I attribute this apparently prejudicial attitude toward Peabody on the part of the Kennedys? I believe it all goes back to when the Irish came to the United States (1845 to 1852) after a long period of drought and poverty in Ireland largely due to a devastating potato famine. In those days, the Yankee Protestants forced the Irish emigres into the most menial jobs as second class citizens. There were signs in the windows stating that Irish Need Not Apply. John Kennedy's father, Joseph P. Kennedy, was one of the first Irishmen who broke out of this prejudicial categorization, went to Harvard, became President of a Massachusetts bank, and went on to become U.S. Ambassador to Great Britain. It is my opinion that this tension continued between the Irish Democrats and the Protestant Republicans of Massachusetts, especially in politics, for too many years.

Yet, at the same time, the Kennedys were extremely protective of their primacy in Massachusetts politics. So, when an outstanding Italian American Democratic Governor of Massachusetts named Foster Furcolo announced that he was going to run for the other Massachusetts U.S. Senate seat then held by the Republican Leverett Saltonstall (the epitome of the Yankee Protestant), the Kennedys gave no support whatsoever to the Furcolo candidacy while never saying a bad word about Saltonstall. Why? Because JFK was not anxious to have another Democrat competing with him for primacy as the Senator from Massachusetts at the same time that he had a very pleasant personal relationship with Saltonstall who had no ambition whatsoever to supplant Kennedy's supremacy in the Senate.

So in this case politics outweighed religious concerns.

Now you have some idea of the complexities of Massachusetts politics.

Another prime example of the competitiveness between the Irish Catholic and the Brahmin (which the dictionary describes as "an aristocratic, highly cultured person, especially one of an old New England family") was the Massachusetts Senate campaign between Henry Cabot Lodge (as Brahmin as you could get) and John F. Kennedy (as Irish Catholic as you could get) in 1952. JFK was only 35 years old at the time. Many observers considered the contest as a grudge match since Lodge's grandfather had defeated Kennedy's grandfather, Boston mayor John F. Fitzgerald (popularly known as "Honey Fitz") for a Senate seat back in 1916. John F. Kennedy squeaked by and upset Lodge, winning the U.S. Senate seat by only 3 percentage points. A similar competition took place in Massachusetts again in 1962 when Ted Kennedy (John Kennedy's kid brother) ran against George Cabot Lodge (Henry Cabot Lodge's son) for John Kennedy's Senate seat (which opened up when JFK became President). It was a hard-fought campaign that brought the Irish Catholic/Yankee Protestant competitiveness to the forefront yet again. Ted was a very effective street level campaigner. I remember campaigning with him one evening. His motor cavalcade stopped right in front of the fancy building where his opponent, George Cabot Lodge lived. Ted climbed up on the back of a truck and, using a megaphone, told the huge crowd that had gathered there to look up at the top floor where, he said, the Cabots lived in elegance among their own while he was down here in the streets where the regular people lived! Ted won the Senate seat, gaining 55 per cent of the vote.

One of my favorite true stories about the Irish Catholic/Yankee Protestant competitiveness concerns the Cabots and the Lowells. A Boston gentleman named Max Kabatznick decided to change his name to "Cabot", so he petitioned the Boston Probate Court for permission to do so legally. The Cabot family then rose up in all its Brahmin wrath and intervened to oppose this upstart who was trying to usurp such a distinguished old Yankee name. The court, however, ruled in favor of Mr. Kabatznick, saying that a person had the right to call himself anything he wished. The next day the <u>Boston Herald</u> published a front page box with a switch on the old quatrain. It read: "For here's to dear old Boston, the home of the bean and the cod, where the Lowells speak only to the Cabots, and the Cabots speak Yiddish by God!"

Today, however, by and large, the almost total dominance of Irish Catholics and Italian Catholics in Massachusetts politics is far less important than it was in the days of JFK. Proof of that contention took place in September of 2018. In a hotly contested Congressional primary election in Massachusetts an African American woman, Ayanna Pressley (formerly a member of the Boston City Council) defeated a long time (20 years to be precise) Italian American, Michael Capuano, for the 7th Massachusetts Congressional District seat in Congress once occupied by none other than John F. Kennedy! I suspect that JFK would have been pleased by this development.

Then Senator John F. Kennedy often would take me with him as he campaigned around the Boston area. As in the case of many wealthy families, the Kennedys were very careful with the dollar. JFK had a clever way of combining generosity with parsimoniousness. Let me explain. While he was a U.S. Senator, Kennedy often would spend long weekends in Massachusetts keeping in close touch with his constituents. One day his office called me and said that the Senator wanted to know whether I would like to accompany him on one of his evening rounds. I readily agreed. That particular day he was visiting constituents in Somerville, which is a thriving working community outside of Boston. To my surprise, our driver pulled up to a much patronized local bar. JFK and I went in, and he immediately bellied up to the bar and ordered a beer for him and one for me. He engaged in conversation with the bartender and the customers. To their surprise and delight, they all came to shake hands with Kennedy...for them, he was "one of the boys". Politically, it was a brilliant appearance. After a second beer for each of us, Kennedy asked for the bill. The bartender handed it to him. JFK took his wallet out of his pocket and handed the bartender the only thing he had in it which was a single one hundred dollar bill and said that that was all he had. The bartender then said that he didn't have change for a hundred...silence...and finally the bartender gracefully said that the beers were "on the house". JFK thanked him profusely and off we went. "That was pretty clever", I said. He just nodded.

The last time Senator John F. Kennedy was in Boston getting ready for the trip to Washington as President of the United States, he told me to be sure to write to him from time to time. I laughed and said: "Sure, I and a million other people...I'm afraid that my letters never will get through to you." "Here's the secret," JFK said. "Be sure to write 'Attention: Evelyn Lincoln' on the envelope and it will be taken out of the mail room and delivered directly to me." (Evelyn was JFK's personal secretary). I did just that, and it worked every time.

Even during his presidential campaign, JFK kept in touch with me. See the attached letter which he signed as "Jack", something he rarely did except for special friends. Also I include here his signed invitation to me to attend his inauguration as President of the United States,

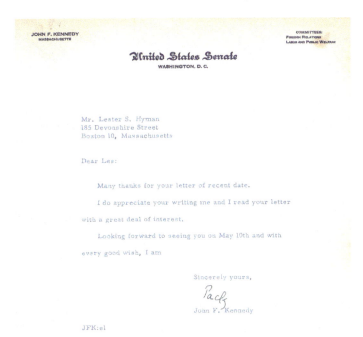

*To Lester Hyman
with best wishes
[signature]*

The Inaugural Committee

*requests the honor of your presence
to attend and participate in the Inauguration of*

John Fitzgerald Kennedy

*as President of the United States of America
and*

Lyndon Baines Johnson

*as Vice President of the United States of America
on Friday the twentieth of January
one thousand nine hundred and sixty-one
in the City of Washington*

Edward H. Foley
Chairman

There always seemed to be a tension in the relationship between President Kennedy and the Governor of Massachusetts Endicott Peabody. Was it the Yankee/Irish problem? I don't really know. Let me give you an example. While still in the White House, John Kennedy was trying to decide where, after he had finished his term of office as President, he wanted his presidential library to be located. Although it ended up in Columbia Point, JFK's first choice at that time was at his alma mater, Harvard, specifically a stretch of property along Boston's Storrow Drive near the Harvard Business School. On one of his trips to Boston, the President asked another Harvard graduate, Governor Endicott Peabody, to join him in looking over property as a possible site for his presidential library. I was delighted when the President insisted that I be in the limousine with the two of them (to keep them apart?). When we arrived at the site, the two men got out of the car to walk the area and look at prospective sites.

When they returned to the car, the Governor held the door for the President. JFK didn't move. "No, *you* get in first, Governor", said the President. "Oh, no," said Peabody politely, "after *you,* Mr. President." Kennedy stood there impatiently and then asked Chub (the Governor) whether he ever had taken a course in accounting which seemed to me to be a rather strange question to ask. The Governor allowed that he had. "So," said the President, "did you ever hear of the accounting term "LIFO"? Chub was perplexed as to the relevance but acknowledged that he had. "Well, that's how it works for the President: He's always 'Last In and First Out' of the automobile. "Now get in, Governor!"

On another occasion I was with the President in his limo...he was late for an engagement so the Secret Service driver was speeding through the town of Brighton. We passed a Catholic Church...all the nuns were lined up on the front walk craning for a look at their beloved Jack Kennedy when, instead of slowing down as the President wished, the driver speeded up and we zoomed by. "Oh, my God," moaned the President, "we're going to kill a nun...that' s all I need".

A second unhappy meeting involving Governor Peabody took place at the Hyannis, Massachusetts Airport. President Kennedy loved Cape Cod and would spend weekends at his home in Hyannisport whenever he possibly could. The Governor, out of politeness, thought it was his duty to greet the President whenever he came back to Massachusetts. So every time the plane touched down at Hyannis Airport, there was Governor Peabody waiting to meet the tired President who didn't want to be greeted...all he wanted was to go home, put his feet up, and relax.

In order to appreciate this story, you have to know about Edwin O'Connor's classic novel of Boston politics "The Last Hurrah". There were all sorts of colorful characters in the book. One in particular was the Boston Fire Commissioner who was portrayed as a somewhat dimwitted fellow who had an unfortunate lisp.

On the particular day of which I speak, the Governor and Mrs. Peabody insisted that I accompany them to Hyannis Airport for their usual greeting of the President, especially because Chub knew that the President had a special relationship with me. When the plane touched down, Chub graciously suggested that I go over to the plane and greet the

President as he came down the stairs and make him aware of the Governor and the First Lady's presence. I did. Kennedy gave me a warm greeting, a few pleasant words, and then looked up to see Chub and Toni Peabody hurrying across the tarmac with big smiles on their faces, ready to greet the President of the United States. Kennedy's look of distaste was obvious, at least to me. But, as always, he subsumed his feelings and expressed them in ironic humor. He leaned over to me and whispered: "Leshta, here comes the Fire Comitthioner!"

Since I mentioned Ed O'Connor, the author of "The Last Hurrah", let me tell you about his wake. In the old days, a good old-fashioned Irish wake was an occasion for celebration as the dear departed is helped off to heaven by a gathering of friends and relatives who eat and drink, often in the presence of the corpse.

When author O'Connor died, tragically young, his wake was a more staid affair. The mourners were a cross-section of Boston and national society: politicians, literary figures, actors, lawyers, doctors and businessmen. One of the theatrical contingent present was Abe Burrows (who directed "Guys and Dolls", "Hello Dolly" and so many other hits) who had a home on Cape Cod where he was friendly with author Ed O'Connor and his wife Vinette. Abe was a big, bald man with an infectious smile, a gravelly voice, and an absurd sense of humor. (when he was younger, Abe was famous for his eccentric musical compositions such as "The Girl with the Three Blue Eyes"). You also have to know that Abe despised Kevin Kelly, the aesthetic, elitist, bitchy theater critic of the Boston Globe. When Kevin disliked a particular artist's work, no matter how successful that artist, Kevin always would trash his work with a snide and carping review. Abe Burrows was one such object of Kevin's derision. He particularly savaged Abe's production of "Breakfast at Tiffanys" when it opened in Boston.

At one point in the proceedings, the four of us were lined up in front of the bier. Abe Burrows, lawyer Bob DeGiacomo, the widow and I. We all looked down at poor Ed – there was a moment of silence – then the irrepressible Abe couldn't stand it any longer. In a rather loud stage whisper, he peered into the coffin and said: "Oh, Eddie, if only that were Kevin Kelly in there instead of you!". It broke up the wake.

Whenever President Kennedy came to Massachusetts, there almost always was a bit of political jostling as to who would be there to greet him as he descended from his plane. Here is a photo showing one of those welcoming committees. Behind Kennedy on the right is (partially shown) Congressman Eddie Boland, and on the left is Attorney-General Frank Bellotti, Speaker of the U.S. House Thomas P. "Tip" O'Neill looking askance, Peabody Press Secretary Jim Smith, and yours truly. I always got a kick out of the fact that JFK greeted me first.

When I was The Assistant to the Governor of Massachusetts - and later when I became Massachusetts Secretary of Commerce and Development - I often had to appear as the guest on radio press conferences. One day I was interviewed by the Boston Globe's distinguished chief political journalist Robert Healy, who had become a friend of mine over the years, but who always asked me very tough (but fair) questions on his radio show. I would say: "Bob, let me say this about that..." and launch into my explanation. After one of these programs, I received a telephone call from Senator Kennedy who happened to be in Boston at the time and heard the show. "Leshtah", he said, "you did a very good job on Bob Healy's radio interview program last night, but I have a suggestion for you. Next time don't keep addressing Healey as "Bob" because people will think it's a set-up between two good personal friends (which was true). If, however, you call him "Mr. Healy", people will think that you're at arm's length, and therefore you'll be more effective and more credible." Today, of course, everyone on the radio and TV talk shows, whether friend or foe, calls each other by their first name whether they really are friends or enemies.

Another time JFK suggested to me that, even though I would explain on talk shows or TV interviews how the Republican Party was ignoring the real needs of the Massachusetts electorate, I should, from time to time, congratulate the Republicans if they did something, even some little thing, that we thought was right. In that way, said Kennedy, the listener will pay more attention when you talk about the Republican "wrongs". By somewhat balancing your comments, you thus make your critical arguments more credible than if you always said the Republicans were doing bad things all the time. Good advice which I readily followed.

Another time Senator Kennedy invited me to come to a big State Democratic dinner where he was scheduled to speak. Because he was the main attraction, he was saved for the very last speaker. Unfortunately it seemed then that every officeholder in the Commonwealth droned on and on before Kennedy was introduced. Finally, JFK was introduced to great cheers as he came to the podium. He then spoke for exactly three minutes...the audience cheered...and that was the end of the dinner. Afterwards we got together and I asked him why he gave such a short address. Kennedy said to me: "Leshtah, it's better to keep them wanting for more instead of giving them too much after so many boring speeches." I thought that was darn good advice.

I learned long ago that writing lengthy speeches takes far less time than writing short speeches. In a lengthy speech, you can develop a theme leisurely and illustrate it with dramatic examples. But with a very short speech, every word has to count. My favorite short speech was written for Governor Peabody to commemorate the 50th anniversary of the ground-breaking of Boston College. President Kennedy was the principal speaker and Governor Peabody was allowed a brief welcoming speech that was not to exceed three minutes in length. And when Kenny O'Donnell, the President's chief assistant, said three minutes, he meant precisely that: 3 minutes and no more...or else. I worked on the Governor's remarks day after day but couldn't seem to come up with anything that would grab the audience's interest in the brief moment assigned to him. I kept researching the history of B.C. looking for an idea. Then I found it. So in the brief speech that Governor Peabody gave, he commented on how appropriate it was that President Kennedy was present because, fifty years earlier, the President's grandfather, "Honey Fitz" Fitzgerald, then the Mayor of Boston, stood in the same spot as we were then and personally laid the cornerstone of Boston College. No one had been aware of this arcane bit of college history, but it "made" the Governor's speech. I was happy in my anonymity, but I had underestimated John F. Kennedy. After the ceremony, we all were in the disrobing room with the Governor and his aides on one side of the room and the President and his people very much on the other side of the room - when the President sent an aide over to our side to say that the President wished to see me right away. I wondered what I had done now. Kennedy said: "Leshtah, that was a very nice speech that the Governor gave." "I'm delighted that you liked it," I said. "But", said the President, "tell me how you knew that my grandfather had laid the cornerstone because my people didn't have that information." "A lot of research," I responded. "Well, thanks for writing such a nice speech", the President said. "It was the Governor's speech," I loyally remarked. "Uh, huh", said the President with a wink. It made my day.

In late 1963, as the Kennedy people prepared for the 1964 re-election campaign, it became obvious that Barry Goldwater would be the likely Republican nominee for President. One day I received a call from Mike Feldman who was President Kennedy's Legal Counsel. He told me that the President was aware of my speech-writing abilities (see the speech at the commemoration of the founding of Boston College) and wanted me to try my hand at a speech he could use when next he came to Massachusetts regarding his putative Republican opponent. Naturally I was thrilled at the assignment and worked as hard as I could on remarks for the President and sent them along to the White House in care of Mike Feldman.

Basically it was a reasoned critique of what we deemed to be the extremist views of Senator Goldwater. A few days later I received a call from Mike...I was hopeful that my draft speech was something that President Kennedy could use. The President appreciated your suggested speech, said Mike, and wanted you to know that it was very well researched and written. I was ecstatic. But, Mike said, the President cannot use it! I was distraught. Then he relayed to me President Kennedy's comment that we should not give Goldwater credibility by analyzing and rebutting his views. Mike said that what President Kennedy decided to do with a far right Republican candidate like Goldwater was not to take him seriously but rather ridicule him with humor. In that way you're showing the voter that Goldwater was not someone to be taken seriously. That piece of advice came in very handy in the years ahead.

President Kennedy had a delicious sense of humor, slightly ironic and totally spontaneous.

Function of Humor

It is said that humor is one of the most effective literary weapons to please the audience, as it develops characters and makes plots useful and memorable. Humor plays many functions in a literary work. It arouses interest among readers, sustains their attention, helps them connect with the characters, emphasizes and relates ideas, and helps the readers picture the situation. Through this tool, writers can also improve the quality of their works by pleasing the audience. *Apart from that, the most dominant function of humor is to provide surprise, which not only improves quality, but improves memorable style of a literary piece.* The writers learn how to use words for different objectives. President Kennedy often used humor effectively, especially in his press conferences. Here are a number of such examples.

March 8, 1961:

Q. I am sure you are aware, sir, of the tremendous mail response that your news conferences on television and radio have produced. There are many Americans who believe that that in our manner of questioning or seeking your attention that we are subjecting you to some abuse or a lack of respect. I wonder, sir, in this light, could you tell us generally your feelings about your press conferences to date and your feelings about how they were conducted?

The President: Well, you subject me to some abuse, but not to any lack of respect. (Laughter)

November 29, 1961

Q. (by the inimitable May Craig) Mr. President, you and your wife and other members of your family have declined to go to private clubs and to take part in other functions, even women's benefits at churches where there was racial segregation. Now I wonder if you don't think it's simply fair that the President of the United States, members of his Cabinet, U.S. Ambassadors and other officers of this Government should decline to speak and participate in functions where women newspaper reporters are banned?

The President: I feel that I have many responsibilities and the press has less and I would think that the press should deal with that problem, and I'm sure that – I think it would be most appropriate if the members of the Press Club had a meeting and permitted you to come and present your views to them. (Laughter)

January 31, 1962

Q. Mr. President, Congressman Alger of Texas today criticized Mr. Salinger (Pierre Salinger who was the President's Press Secretary) as a "young and inexperienced White House publicity man" and questioned the advisability of having him visit the Soviet Union. I wonder if you have any comments.

The President. I know there are always some people who feel that Americans are always young and inexperienced, and foreigners are always able and tough and great negotiators, But I don't think that the United States would have acquired its present position of leadership in the free world if that view were correct. Now he also, as I saw in the press, said that Mr. Salinger's main job was to increase my standing in the Gallup polls. Having done that, he is now moving on to improve our communications. (Laughter)

March 10, 1962 (at a fund-raising dinner in honor of Senator George Smathers)

The President. "I regard him as one of my most valuable counselors in a moment of great personal and public difficulty. In 1952, when I was thinking about running for the United States Senate, I went to the then Senator Smathers and said "George, what do you think?" He said: "Don't do it. Can't win. Bad year." I won. In 1956 I was at the Democratic Convention, and I said – I didn't know whether I would run for Vice President or not - so I said, "George, what do you think? This is it. They need a young man. "It's your chance," he said. So I ran – and lost. And in 1960 I was wondering whether I ought to run in the West Virginia primary. "Don't do it", he said. That State you can't possibly carry." And actually the only time I really got nervous about the whole matter at Los Angeles (the Democratic National Convention) was just before the balloting for President, and George came up and he said: "I think it looks pretty good for you".

February 21, 1963

Q. Mr. President, the practice of managed news is attributed to your administration. Mr. Salinger says that he has never had it defined. Would you give us your definition and tell us why you find it necessary to practice it?

The President. You are charging us with something, Ms. Craig, and then you are asking me to define what it is you are charging me with. I think that you might – let me just say we've had very limited success in managing the news, if that's what we've been trying to do. Perhaps you would tell us what it is you object to in our treatment of the news.

Q. You are asking me, sir?
The President. Yes.
Q. Well, I don't believe in managed news at all. I thought we ought to get everything we want.
The President.
Well, I think that you should too, Mrs. Craig. I am for that. (Laughter)

May 22, 1963

Q. Mr. President, Governor Rockefeller, Governor Romney and Senator Goldwater, none of these gentlemen are willing to admit that they are candidates in 1964. I wonder if to your experienced eye any of them looks like a candidate, and would you be a little more frank than they are about your plans?

The President. If I had to, I would say that if the party, if the spirit of the party comes to them that they will answer the call in all three cases, and I would say that is about my position, too. Laughter

At one of the press conferences, May Craig asked the President if he enjoyed being President and would he recommend it to others. His brief response was: "Yes as to the first. No, as to the second.

When JFK received an Honorary Degree of Doctor of Laws on June 11, 1962 at Yale University, he opened his speech by saying: "It might be said that I have the best of both worlds, a Harvard education and a Yale degree."

Whenever Massachusetts had a problem that required the help of the President, normally the Governor of the State would go to Washington to consult with the White House. Governor Peabody, however, felt that there was not a close personal relationship between himself and President Kennedy. Perhaps it had something to do with the age-old friction between the Irish Catholics and the Yankee Protestants in Massachusetts. Governor Peabody, to his credit, wanted to do whatever would bring about a positive result for his State so, leaving ego aside, he felt it would be better from time to time for me to handle Massachusetts political business with the White House because of my close personal relationship with President Kennedy. So I would go to Washington and meet with the President's chief staffers, Ken O'Donnell and Larry O'Brien, to discuss whatever political problems Massachusetts had. It was heady stuff. On one occasion, I just had completed my business with Ken and Larry when Ken asked me if I would like to say hello to the President. "Could I?" I said. "Of course, he likes you," said Ken. He then took me into the Oval Office, and there was President Kennedy seated behind his desk. He looked up and greeted me with: "Leshtah, you get out of heah, you're the kiss of death". I was completely taken aback. "I don't understand Mr. President," I said, "What have I done?" And he said: "I told you to work for Eddie McLaughlin for Congress. You did ...and he lost. I told you to work for Johnny Powers for Mayor...you did, and he lost." He then rattled off three more people he had told me to support, and they, too, all had lost. "I'm running for re-election next year" continued the President, "and you're the kiss of death. So you get out of here." I didn't know what to do, so I turned around and headed for the door. "Come back, come back," he said, "I was just kidding." Then he roared with laughter as I realized that he was tweaking me and wasn't at all serious.

That was the last time I saw JFK until his untimely death.

With regard to Kennedy's vaunted sense of humor, I attach his favorite quote from the Ramayana:

ON APRIL 25, 1962 PRESIDENT KENNEDY GAVE DAVE POWERS, HIS SPECIAL ASSISTANT AND LONGTIME CONFIDANT, A SILVER BEER MUG FOR A BIRTHDAY PRESENT WITH THE FOLLOWING INSCRIPTION:

There are three things which are real;
God, Human Folly and Laughter.
The first two are beyond our comprehension
So we must do what we can with the third.

John. F. Kennedy

... from "The Ramayana" by Aubrey Mennen.

Back in the Fifties when I first came to Washington, there was very little night life. There was no Kennedy Center...maybe two or three first-rate restaurants...a burlesque house...and a segregated Lincoln Theater (as a young lawyer at the SEC and a lover of good music, I once went to the Lincoln Theater to hear the great Ethel Waters sing. The next morning I was called into my boss's office at the SEC and informed that I was never to go to the Lincoln Theater again because it was located in an area of D.C. that was solely for black people. I rebelled and said I would go wherever I wished). Perhaps I was before my time. Today, of course, Washington is a fully integrated city. President Kennedy capsulized it all when he said, tongue in cheek: "Washington is a city of northern charm and southern efficiency".

On November 21, 1963 the Governor of Massachusetts, Endicott "Chub" Peabody, told me that he was going to take the next day off in order to go to Gettysburg, Pennsylvania for a Civil War commemoration and private tour of the battlefield...and would I like to come with him. I begged off because frankly I was exhausted in my job as The Assistant to the Governor and wanted to take this rare opportunity to be home with my family. He kindly understood and agreed.

The next morning I was doing some errands near my home in Marshfield, Massachusetts which is about 30 miles south of Boston listening to music on the car radio when the broadcast was interrupted with the horrifying news that President Kennedy apparently had been shot while he was riding in a motorcade in Dallas, Texas and was now on his way to Parkland Hospital.

Shocked by this news, I literally drove my car off the road and into some dense undergrowth which prevented any serious damage. I sat there...numb...trying to grasp the enormity of what had happened and praying for the best. Within minutes, the words I had dreaded were spoken: the President was dead. It was as if the bottom had fallen out of my life. This man whom I revered as a patron, a President...and a friend...was no more. I got my car back on the road, returned to my home, and learned that the Governor was flying back from Pennsylvania and wanted me to join him. Not knowing how long I would be in Boston, I quickly packed a suitcase and headed back to the State House. All of Massachusetts ... indeed all of the nation and the world...was in deep shock. I helped the Governor write a proclamation marking the tragedy while he ordered all the flags of the Commonwealth to be lowered to half-staff immediately. Here's what I wrote: "Our President is dead. It is difficult for all of us who knew John F. Kennedy so long and so well to comprehend this tragic fact. He now belongs to eternity. But the world will long feel the impact of his presence on this earth. His contributions to humanity were many. Our hearts go out to the parents, the wife, and the children of our beloved President. May our prayers be with them to sustain and comfort them in their darkest hour. We must now rededicate ourselves to those principles which President Kennedy championed so nobly, and for which he gave the ultimate sacrifice, his life. The greatest tribute we can offer to his memory is our continued pursuit of a world where all men may live together in peace and freedom."

OUR PRESIDENT IS DEAD. IT IS DIFFICULT FOR ALL OF US WHO KNEW JOHN F. KENNEDY SO LONG AND SO WELL TO COMPREHEND THIS TRAGIC FACT. HE NOW BELONGS TO ETERNITY. BUT THE WORLD WILL LONG FEEL THE IMPACT OF HIS PRESENCE ON THIS EARTH. HIS CONTRIBUTIONS TO HUMANITY WERE MANY

ON A ~~MORE PERSONAL LEVEL~~, OUR HEARTS GO OUT TO THE PARENTS, THE WIFE, AND THE CHILDREN OF OUR BELOVED PRESIDENT. MAY OUR PRAYERS BE WITH THEM TO SUSTAIN AND COMFORT THEM IN THEIR DARKEST HOUR.

WE MUST NOW REDEDICATE OURSELVES TO THOSE PRINCIPLES WHICH PRESIDENT KENNEDY CHAMPIONED SO NOBLY, AND FOR WHICH HE GAVE THE ULTIMATE SACRIFICE, HIS LIFE. THE GREATEST TRIBUTE WE CAN OFFER TO HIS MEMORY IS OUR CONTINUED PURSUIT OF A WORLD WHERE ALL MEN MAY LIVE TOGETHER IN PEACE AND FREEDOM.

In a few days, I joined Governor Peabody in Washington for the funeral (see the program attached).

FUNERAL SERVICES OF
JOHN FITZGERALD KENNEDY
LATE PRESIDENT OF THE UNITED STATES
MONDAY, NOVEMBER 25, 1963

Procession departs the Capitol at 11:00 A.M.

Mrs. Kennedy and The Attorney General in an automobile will join the military formation to proceed to the White House.

Members of Congress who will participate in the funeral ceremonies (except The Leadership)* will proceed directly to St. Matthew's Cathedral to be seated by 11:45 A.M.

The military formation will proceed down Pennsylvania Avenue past the White House and pause in the intersection of 17th and Pennsylvania. In the meantime, the caisson will have entered the North East Gate and proceed to the North Portico, followed by Mrs. Kennedy and The Attorney General. They will leave the automobile at this point and be joined by the other dignitaries who will proceed with them on foot behind the caisson. The caisson will move forth and the procession will proceed to St. Matthew's via Connecticut Avenue.

The following will assemble at the White House at 11:15 A.M. preparatory to joining Mrs. Kennedy and Family on the walk from the White House to the Cathedral:

       The President
       Chiefs of State, Heads of Government and
           Chiefs of Special Delegations
       The Chief Justice
       Former Presidents
       Justices of the Supreme Court
       Members of the Cabinet
       Congressional Leadership
       The Joint Chiefs of Staff
       Personal Assistants to President Kennedy
       Close friends

Those who are not in the procession but who have been invited to attend the Requiem Mass at the Cathedral should proceed directly to the Cathedral and be in their places at approximately 11:45 A.M. ADMISSION WILL BE BY INVITATION ONLY AND CARDS OF ADMISSION WILL BE GIVEN TO THOSE PARTICIPATING IN THE CEREMONIES.

Upon the conclusion of the ceremonies at the Cathedral, those attending the Mass enter their cars and join the procession from the Cathedral to Arlington National Cemetery in the following order of precedence:

      Mrs. Kennedy and Members of the immediate family
      The President and his Party
      Chiefs of State, Heads of Government and Chiefs of
         Special Delegations
      The Chief Justice of the Supreme Court
      Dean of the Diplomatic Corps
      Justices of the Supreme Court
      Members of the Cabinet
      Leadership of the Senate
      Governors of the States and Territories
      Leadership of the House of Representatives
      Joint Chiefs of Staff
      Personal Staff of President Kennedy
      Close friends of the family

Others attending the funeral mass are invited to Arlington Cemetery.

The procession upon arrival at the site of interment will halt and passengers will leave their automobiles and proceed to the grave site. After the interment ceremonies, those participating will return to their cars and return to the city.

Governors of the States and Territories are requested to provide their own transportation to the Cathedral. After the services transportation will be provided to Arlington National Cemetery and from there to Washington, D.C.

* The Congressional Leadership who have been invited to join Mrs. Kennedy, along with others, in a walk from the White House will assemble at the White House (Diplomatic entrance) at 11:30 A.M.

JOHN FITZGERALD KENNEDY
President of the United States
May 29, 1917 – November 22, 1963

Dear God,
    Please take care of your servant
        John Fitzgerald Kennedy

Now the trumpet summons us again—not as a call to bear arms, though arms we need—not as a call to battle, though embattled we are—but a call to bear the burden of a long twilight struggle, year in and year out, "rejoicing in hope, patient in tribulation"—a struggle against the common enemies of man: tyranny, poverty, disease and war itself . . .

In the long history of the world, only a few generations have been granted the role of defending freedom in its hour of maximum danger. I do not shrink from this responsibility—I welcome it. I do not believe that any of us would exchange places with any other people or any other generation. The energy, the faith, the devotion which we bring to this endeavor will light our country and all who serve it—and the glow from that fire can truly light the world . . .

With a good conscience our only sure reward, with history the final judge of our deeds, let us go forth to lead the land we love, asking His blessing and His help, but knowing that here on earth God's work must truly be our own.

We stayed at the Mayflower Hotel on Connecticut Avenue along with many of the top officials of the Commonwealth. We huddled together in the living-room of the Governor's suite, comforting one another and trying to figure out whether it was a large-scale conspiracy or the act of a single crazed gunman. We were sure that when the Dallas police questioned Lee Harvey Oswald, we would have the answers. The television set was playing constantly as we watched the sad drama unfold. Suddenly the Speaker of the Massachusetts House, John Thompson, called our attention to the scene on the TV screen as Oswald was being moved through a corridor. Before our very eyes - live - we saw Jack Ruby emerge from the shadows and pump three bullets into Oswald. Speaker Thompson began to sob. Our shock deepened - all of this was totally unbelievable.

The next day, just before the funeral service at the Cathedral, the Governor went out for a brief walk, and I was sitting alone in our suite when the phone rang. I answered. It was George Wallace, the controversial governor of Alabama. I told him that Peabody was out taking a walk, and then Wallace asked if I would come up to his room and sit with him for a while…that he wanted to talk with me about something. I thought it a curious request but decided to honor it. When I got there, there was only one other person in the room with Wallace (a professional humorist who was an old friend of Wallace's).

The Governor wanted me to know that, although he had been "pretty rough" on President Kennedy in his rhetoric, he liked him very much personally and was distraught by his assassination. I said that I believed him.

Then he asked me to come over to his clothes closet. That baffled me until Wallace explained that he was just a "country boy" and wasn't sure that he had brought the proper clothes to wear at a state funeral...and would I please look at his clothes and tell me if they were acceptable. He was like a kid who didn't know what to wear to the prom. I did...and they were.

Then he got around to the real purpose of the visit. "Les," he said, "would you please do me a favor and pick up my ticket for the funeral service at the Cathedral at the same time that you pick up Governor Peabody's ticket?"

"Why can't you or your people do that, Governor", I asked. "Well, if they see me," said Wallace, "knowing how I criticized Jack Kennedy so much, they might not give me a ticket for the funeral. But they'd probably give it to you because you are a Kennedy person."

"Governor", I responded, "with all respect, you're not here as George Wallace. You're here as the Governor of the State of Alabama, and they'll give you your ticket because of the high office that you hold."

That didn't seem to satisfy Wallace and he kept pressing until finally I agreed to pick up his ticket at the same time I went to call for Governor Peabody's ticket. That is exactly what I did, but when I tried to deliver the ticket to Wallace, I was told that he had had a change of heart and had gotten the ticket himself. So there was one extra ticket outstanding, and I had it.

Later I was told that all the tickets were collected at the church as people came in to be seated and that then all of them had been destroyed. But I still have in my possession that extra ticket which I believe to be the only admission pass to the funeral of John F. Kennedy in existence ...thanks to, of all people, George Corley Wallace.

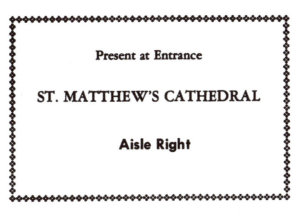

Leaders from all over the world poured into Washington to honor our fallen President. The entire Kennedy family, followed by dignitaries from various countries, marched slowly up Connecticut Avenue on to St. Matthews Cathedral where the funeral was held. Governor Peabody and I and our State trooper Ed Teahan stood on a little balcony over the front entrance of the Mayflower Hotel watching below as the Kennedy family and leaders from all over the world including the 6'5" tall Charles DeGaulle marching up Connecticut Avenue next to the 5'2" Lion of Judah, Hailie Selassie of Ethiopia. It was a bitter cold day, and the Governor's State Trooper Ed Teahan, concerned that I would catch a cold, thoughtfully gave me his own overcoat to keep warm. Down below, all along Connecticut Avenue, Secret Service men carried pistols and machine guns, constantly scanning the buildings along the parade route. I put my hand in Captain

Teahan's coat pocket for warmth and felt a solid object which I pulled out to see what it was. It was Teahan's service revolver! In a flash his hand chopped down on mine, forcing me to drop the gun onto the floor of the balcony. I was petrified. Eddie apologized and pointed out that, if the Secret Service men marching along the parade group had seen me holding a pistol while heads of state marched by, they would have shot first and asked questions later. I was shaking for the rest of the procession...and not from the cold. Cardinal Cushing presided over the funeral mass at the Cathedral and again at the burial ceremony at Arlington National Cemetery. Soon it was over. And a traumatized nation tried to get used to the fact that Jack Kennedy was gone and Lyndon B. Johnson now was our President.

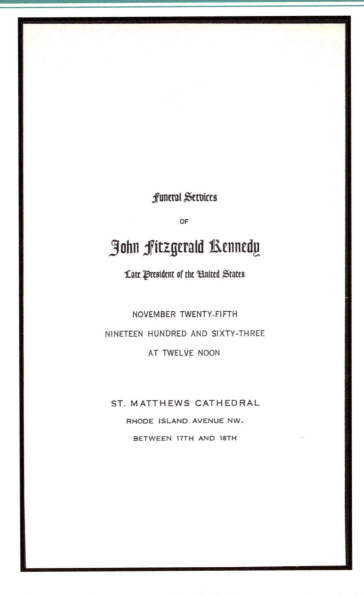

After President Kennedy died, it was as though I had lost a member of my family. I didn't know what to do or how to express my grief. The best I could think of to demonstrate my feelings was to write to both Bobby and Ted expressing my condolences...which I did. Surely I did not expect a reply from either of the brothers because, undoubtedly, hundreds, if not thousands, of friends, officials and admirers from all over the world were doing exactly the same as I. Thus you can imagine my surprise and appreciation when I received a hand-signed "thank you" note from each of the brothers, which meant so much to me as almost a member of the family.

> *We are deeply touched by your thoughtfulness in letting us know that you share in our sorrow.*
>
> *We are consoled by the knowledge that the love he gave is returned in full measure.*
>
> Dear Les,
> My thanks for your letter
>
> *Robert and Ethel Kennedy*

Dear Ly -

Our heartfelt appreciation for your thoughtfulness

and your prayers

Senator and Mrs. Edward M. Kennedy

Ted / Joan.

Throughout this book, I have given examples of JFK's delightful sense of humor.

Ironically, on the very last day of his life...November 22, 1963...President Kennedy began his day with a speech at a breakfast gathering at the Fort Worth, Texas Chamber of Commerce as follows: "Two years ago I introduced myself in Paris by saying that I was the man who accompanied Mrs. Kennedy to Paris. I am getting somewhat the same sensation as I travel around Texas. Nobody wonders what Lyndon and I wear!" A few hours later he was gone.

Ten years later, on November 22, 1973. Ted Kennedy paid tribute to his fallen older brother as follows: "His appeal summons us anew – not merely to remember him but to rededicate ourselves. *The unfinished quality of his life symbolizes the unfinished agenda of America.* And as the torch is passed to each succeeding generation, I believe that those who seek peace and justice, those who join the forward march of the human pilgrimage on earth, will say of John Fitzgerald Kennedy: He has never left us – and he never will." To which I say: Amen

America lost a President, and I lost a dear and valued friend. I would like to think that John Fitzgerald Kennedy would have been proud of my career in law and politics. One of the ways in which I honor my friendship with President Kennedy is by acting as a mentor to other young people, just as JFK did for me. Another way has been my involvement in promoting civil rights (especially voting rights which was such a key issue for the then Senator Kennedy) for *all* Americans. Let me give you one example of the latter. In 1966, three years after President Kennedy died, I was asked by my old friend Charles Evers, the first African-American Mayor of Fayette, Mississippi since Reconstruction, and brother of civil rights icon Medgar Evers, to come to Mississippi where, as an attorney, I tried civil rights cases in courts where people of color were being denied the right to vote. I returned to Mississippi again in 1969 to help Charles who was running for Governor of that state and spoke to groups in and around the Natchez area. I write about this only because, without my knowledge and to my surprise, signs were posted at all the black churches where I spoke on Charles' behalf saying: "Come hear friend of John F. Kennedy speak"...that was me. I trust that JFK would have been pleased.

Snapshots of the Kennedys

Rose Kennedy

Rose Fitzgerald Kennedy
1890-1995

The day after I met Rose Kennedy for the first time at a dinner in honor of Senator Edward M. Kennedy, I told Ted that it was a pleasure to have met his mother and what a sweet person she is. He looked at me somewhat askance and said: "My mother 'sweet'…are you kidding?" He then proceeded to tell me the following story.

One day Mrs. Kennedy was contacted by a man named Ollie Cohen who ran a very popular store in Boston called

King's Discount. He knew that Mrs. Kennedy was very active in raising funds for the Kennedy Foundation that helped mentally challenged children. One of her ways of doing this was to have the Foundation sell what they called "Candles of Hope" with the proceeds going to the foundation.

Ollie decided that he could help her, as well as himself. He told Mrs. Kennedy that he would sell the Candles of Hope in his store for a week, with all of the proceeds from those sales going to the Kennedy Foundation providing that Mrs. Kennedy act as the salesperson on the first day. She readily agreed and Ollie was delighted.

He immediately called the Boston press corps to alert them to come to his store to see Rose Kennedy "in person" selling her Candles of Hope, knowing that this would be terrific publicity for his store.

On the appointed day and time, reporters, photographers, and TV cameras all showed up at the King Discount store. Ollie was ecstatic. Soon a limousine pulled up to the rear door of the store and Mr. Cohen hurried there in order to greet Mrs. Kennedy and escort her to the front of the store where the press could observe her selling the candles. What a photo op that would be! Ollie told Mrs. Kennedy how thrilled he was to have her do this. She looked Mr. Cohen right in the eye and said: "I'm so pleased that you're going to give *the total receipts of your entire store for the week* to the Kennedy Foundation."

And Ollie said: "You don't understand, Mrs. Kennedy, it's the receipts *just for the sale of the candles* that are going to your Foundation." "I'm afraid *you* don't understand, Mr. Cohen," she said. "It's the total receipts of your <u>entire</u> store for a week that will go to the Foundation...and if you don't want to do that, I'll just turn around and go home."

Ollie had been had. He couldn't fail to produce Rose Kennedy for the press corps, so reluctantly he agreed to Mrs. Kennedy's terms...and a lot of money went to the Kennedy Foundation.

"And that," Ted said to me, "is my sweet mother."

* * *

Robert Francis Kennedy

In mid-April 1968 I was on the road much of the time on behalf of Robert F. Kennedy's campaign for the presidency of the United States. On one weekend, however, I managed to get back to our home in Waban, Massachusetts for a weekend with the family. When I arrived, I found that my oldest son David, then 8 years old, had been involved in a fight at school and had come home with a black eye. I questioned David about the incident and found out that he had fought with one of the other children in his class about politics. Most of the children in David's public school lived in Newton, Massachusetts which, along with Brookline, were probably the two most liberal towns in Massachusetts. Almost all of the parents were vociferously supporting Eugene McCarthy for President. David was the only child in his class who was for Bobby Kennedy, and amazingly, tempers ran high especially among the children, many of whom reflected their parents' views...and Dave got into a fight.

I told David that just because I was supporting Bobby Kennedy, that did not mean that he had to support him and that it would be a lot easier for him to support Senator McCarthy in order to maintain peace in his classroom. I am proud to say that David flatly refused. "I'm for Bobby Kennedy, Dad", he said, "and I'm not going to change".

Back on the road again, I was with Bobby one evening and, in a rare moment of privacy, I told him what had happened with my son and asked him whether he ever had such problems with *his* kids. Bobby gave me that cold Kennedy stare, said "yes, yes" and walked off. I was furious. What an insensitive son-of-a-bitch, I thought to myself.

The following weekend, however, when I was home again for a few hours, David came bursting into the library where I was catching up on correspondence and proudly waved a letter under my nose. It was addressed to David A. Hyman and read as follows: "Dear David, Your Dad tells me that you're my biggest booster in your class and I just wanted you to know how much I appreciate it. Thanks very much for your support, David, and I hope I'll have the pleasure of thanking you in person one day soon. Your friend, Robert F. Kennedy." David was thrilled, and so was I.

LESTER S. HYMAN

ROBERT F. KENNEDY
NEW YORK

United States Senate
WASHINGTON, D.C. 20510

April 26, 1968

Dear David:

Your Dad tells me that you're my biggest booster in your class and I just wanted you to know how much I appreciate it.

Thanks very much for your support, David, and I hope I'll have the pleasure of thanking you in person one day soon.

Your friend,

Robert F. Kennedy

Master David Hyman
c/o Lester S. Hyman
11 Beacon Street
Boston, Massachusetts 02108

Th next time I caught up with Bobby on the road, I confronted him about the incident. "I don't understand", I said, "why you were so cold when I asked you about my son's fight in school and then you turned around and wrote him

86

such a gorgeous letter?" Bob replied: "It's simple. *You* aren't the problem...your kid is". That made sense, I thought. Then he told me that he would be coming to Boston in July for a speech at the Park Plaza Hotel. He suggested that I get a room there, put my son David in it by himself, give him (Bobby) the key and he would spend some time alone with my son after he finished his speech. What a lovely gesture. But, as the world knows to its regret, he never made it. Robert F. Kennedy was assassinated on June 6, 1968.

This incident demonstrates that while RFK sometimes appeared to be a cold, insensitive man, he really was a very emotional and passionat**e** person who carefully hid that side of him so fellow politicians never would think that he was soft.

In 1967, during Bob Kennedy's presidential campaign, he asked me, as my first major assignment on his behalf, to go to the State of Michigan where the Democrats there were preparing for their nominating convention at which delegates would be chosen for the forthcoming *national* convention in Chicago which, in turn, would choose the Democratic candidate for President. At this particular time Bobby was concentrating on key state contests and so he asked my colleague Joe Crangle who then was head of the New York Democratic Party, and I, as Chairman of the Massachusetts Democratic Party, to represent the Kennedys in Michigan which indeed was a key state.

Our chief opponent for earning the delegate support of the Michigan Democrats was Hubert Humphrey who was extremely popular in Michigan. More importantly, Hubert was there in person, while Bobby was not. Thus it was an uphill fight for us. Joe Crangle and I recommended to Ted

Kennedy that he come to Michigan on behalf of his brother so there would be a strong Kennedy presence there. The night before the State convention began, we got a call from Ted telling us that he had decided to take our advice and would fly to Michigan to help us in our quest for delegates. He arrived at 4 in the morning by private plane, and we immediately began to brief him. Ted's back (which he had injured some time ago when a private plane in which he was a passenger crashed) was constantly giving him a great deal of pain, so he soaked in a hot bath tub while Joe and I reviewed campaign strategy with him.

Hubert was scheduled to have breakfast with the leaders of the Michigan Democratic party first thing in the morning hopefully to get their support for *his* candidacy for President. Ted concluded that it would be disruptive, if not rude, if he were to try and attend that meeting himself and challenge Hubert but instead asked me to go and report back to him what Hubert had to say so he later would be prepared to rebut his arguments. I did so. When I got back to Ted's room, he asked me to brief him on what had happened. "Well", I said, "Hubert says that it was he, not President Kennedy, who had thought up the idea for the Peace Corps". "Yes, yes", said Ted, "what else?" "And Hubert said it was he, not President Kennedy, who was really responsible for the non-nuclear proliferation treaty." "Yes, yes, and what else?" And so it went down a long list of achievements that Hubert claimed solely (and inaccurately) for himself. At the conclusion of my briefing, Ted considered the information carefully, looked up at me with that great Kennedy smile, and said: "I'm for him", he joked. When, however, the votes were taken, Bob Kennedy more than held his own by getting the majority of the Michigan delegates. Joe

Crangle and I then received a phone call from Bobby expressing his gratification for the good result we achieved.

From Michigan I moved into the New England states, constantly hunting for RFK delegates. In the meantime, Bobby had suffered a setback at the hands of Eugene McCarthy in the quirky Oregon primary, so now it was on to California which was "make or break". Whichever of the candidates would win California surely would become the Democratic nominee for President of the United States and have an excellent chance of winning the presidency itself.

The night of the California primary, which Bobby Kennedy won, making him almost surely the Democratic candidate for President, I returned home to Massachusetts after an exhausting week on the road, and so my wife and I went to bed very early. A few moments later, just as we had fallen asleep, the telephone awakened us. It was a reporter from one of the local radio stations telling us that Bobby had been shot. I couldn't believe it...it was all so surreal. Right away my wife switched on the television set in time for us to see the pandemonium in Los Angeles. Meanwhile, on the telephone, I could hear the beeps which indicated that our conversation was being recorded. "How bad is it?" I asked. "We don't know yet," said the reporter "but would you please just assume that Robert Kennedy is dead and give us an obituary statement?" For someone who was taught to choose his words carefully especially when talking to the press, I threw caution to the wind and replied: "Go f---- yourself" and hung up. What a premature, ghoulish, and insensitive request he had made. To the reporter's credit, he must have realized what he had done, for he called me in the morning to apologize which I accepted.

All of us were in shock. It was almost too much to fathom. Another Kennedy brother dying violently. First, Joe Jr. in a plane crash; then the President was shot; and now Bobby. Poor Ted now was alone.

We went to New York for the funeral at St. Patrick's Cathedral. I was asked to be one of the Honorary Pallbearers, standing beside the coffin throughout the night as thousands of mourners from all walks of life passed by to pay their respects. The next day we piled into buses to take us to Pennsylvania Station where the funeral train would carry Bobby back to Washington for burial. I was seated in a bus next to civil rights leader Charles Evers who had a portable radio with him. As the bus pulled away from the church, we heard that James Earl Ray had been captured and arraigned as the alleged assassin of Martin Luther King. Charles was incredulous and told me that there was no way that Ray could have committed such a crime alone (but that never has been proved).

The funeral train moved slowly from New York to Washington. Thousands and thousands of people...men, women and children...lined the tracks to honor the fallen Kennedy. There were American flags everywhere. Children stood at attention. Adults saluted. Inside the train it was like an old-fashioned Irish wake. Steve Smith had ordered the bar opened, and people from every phase of Robert Kennedy's life reminisced as the hours went by. My wife and I were seated at a table in the dining car with Shirley McLaine and Sidney Poitier. Shirley kept dabbing at her eyes with a handkerchief that she called her "shmata". Whenever the political stories that we told about the campaign turned humorous, we managed to laugh for a brief moment in the midst of this tragedy, but then suddenly a total silence would come over us as Ethel Kennedy (Bobby's wonderful wife), accompanied by her eldest son Joe (who became a Congressman from Massachusetts), walked through each car of the train to thank everyone for coming and to express appreciation for all we had done to help Bobby. To describe Ethel's courage and self-discipline at that heart-breaking moment, I could think only of a favorite Kennedy word: Gutsy!

Soon after the train's sad journey began, I was asked to come to the rear car where the coffin lay. The family had decided that there were so many people standing along the tracks who wanted to pay tribute to RFK that the coffin should be lifted up so it could be seen through the window. So we placed some chairs in the middle of the train car and lifted the coffin onto them. We then had to hold the coffin steady since the train was swaying back and forth as we traveled. Ivanhoe Donaldson and Peter Edelman and I stood for what seemed like hours holding onto the coffin until another set of friends could replace us. It probably was my imagination, but I felt as though RFK was moving inside...it was an eerie experience. In that car, Ethel Kennedy sat crumpled on the floor in one corner. Andy Williams was there to comfort her, as was Jacqueline Kennedy and Ted Kennedy.

Because there were so many spectators along the track, the Kennedy family asked that the train proceed slowly so everyone could see the coffin. As a result, instead of arriving in Washington by midafternoon for the burial ceremony at Arlington National Cemetery, we did not get there until evening when the sun already had gone down. No one had planned for such an eventuality, and the problem was that the burial service would have to take place in the dark. So Ted Kennedy ran to a nearby church and retrieved all the candles that he could – they were handed to each of us at the burial site – and the service proceeded as hundreds of candles flickered bright and then died, a fitting symbol for the sad duty that we were performing. I still have my two candles which have been preserved under glass and hang in my home office as a reminder of what might have been.

Robert Kennedy, more than most political figures that I have come to know over the years, looked ahead and foresaw what our nation and the world could become. In 1967 he wrote a book called "To Seek a Newer World". In it he called for "a shared determination to wipe away the unnecessary sufferings of our fellow human beings at home and abroad." He went on to say: "Our answer is the world's hope; it is to rely on youth – not a time of life but a state of mind, a temper of the will, a quality of the imagination, a predominance of courage over timidity, of the appetite for adventure over the love of ease. The cruelties and obstacles of this swiftly changing planet will not yield to obsolete dogmas and outworn slogans. It cannot be moved by those who cling to a present that is already dying, who prefer the illusion of security to the excitement and danger that come with even the most peaceful progress. It is a revolutionary world we live in; and this generation, at home and around the world, has had thrust upon it a greater burden of responsibility than any generation that has ever lived." Quite a remarkable challenge for the future.

Edward M. Kennedy

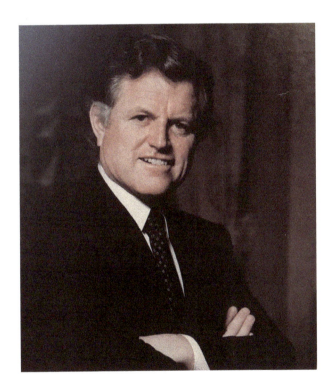

One day when I was in Washington working on my report on the Model Cities program for the U.S. Department of Housing and Urban Development, someone called me from across the room in an excited voice to tell me that Senator Edward M. Kennedy was on the phone for me. As I took the call, a number of my HUD colleagues gathered around me since, to say the least, it was not usual for a member of the United States Senate to call a lowly consultant. Ted went right to the point and asked whether I would like to be the Chairman of the Massachusetts Democratic Party. I said "yes" emphatically, and a new phase of my life opened before me.

It was a tribute to Ted Kennedy's creativity and willingness to take a big chance that I got the job. My predecessors were all good Irishmen (Gerard Doherty, Patsy Lynch, Onions Burke and Charlie McGlue…honest!) Certainly, no Jewish person ever had held the position. Burton Hersh, who wrote the definitive biography of Ted ("The Education of Edward M. Kennedy") said the following about me: "The Chairman of the Massachusetts Democratic Committee and therefore, ipso facto, Edward Kennedy's personal choice to run the Democratic Party was Lester Hyman…When Hyman replaced (Gerard) Doherty, the pros around the State House gazed uniformly with culture shock after years of exposure to Doherty's mudflat personality. Dealing with Hyman was like a stroll through steaming hanging gardens…Careful about his tailoring, he has a way of dealing affectionately on his rich wet vowel sounds that produced in Kennedy headquarters a barrage of anti-Semitic hate notes from denizens of South Boston walk-ups heartsick to believe that the party of James A. Curley and Onions Burke was willingly placed by a fellow Irish in the hands of this reincarnated Disraeli." Wow!

Ted Kennedy announces on radio and television that Lester Hyman will be the new Chairman of the Massachusetts Democratic Party.

Ted and I decided that, as the first order of business, we would put together a Democratic Advisory Council made up of some of the best minds in Massachusetts (and the nation) to come up with exciting new ideas for the Democratic Party. We recruited people like economists Paul Samuelson and John Kenneth Galbraith, the redoubtable Daniel Patrick Moynihan, General James Gavin and Eli Goldston. We met regularly at Ted's Boston town house to develop new ideas for the Party. Out of our deliberations came a Democratic program for the State. The Boston radio station WEEI editorialized: "We are willing to bet that there are few state parties, either Democratic or Republican, that could match such an advisory council in terms of intellect, prestige and the number of concrete sensible proposals it has made."

I particularly remember one evening when Jim Gavin, the courageous former General who led key American forces in Europe on D-Day, looked around the room and said very quietly: "Playgrounds". We looked askance, but then he explained. A great deal of juvenile crime takes place because youngsters don't have anything meaningful to do. After school is over, we lock up the playgrounds so noone can use them. Why not keep them open all day and all evening, asked Jim? He continued: Put in lights so the kids can play sports at night and help keep them out of trouble. At that moment, I submit, the now-popular concept of "night basketball" was born.

The real question was what to do with the Advisory Council's ideas. At the time, the Massachusetts Legislature was, in a sense, a "closed shop". The members took tremendous pride in the institution and jealously guarded it against any intrusion from the outside. In their minds, the U.S. Senator from Massachusetts, the Governor of the State, and especially that upstart young Democratic Party Chairman were very much outsiders.

How could I gain their confidence? I tried by supporting their legislation and their candidacies wherever and whenever in good conscience I could. I traveled constantly around the State, appearing on radio and television shows, call-in programs and visiting the local newspapers and Editorial Board meetings for interviews, addressing citizen groups and the Party faithful, singing the praises of the Great and General Court (the Legislature). It worked. At a time when politics was a dirty word, here was a young, fresh faced non-office holder challenging the conventional wisdom by proclaiming that public service was an honorable profession that deserved respect, and pointing out, chapter and verse, how much the legislators were doing constructively to help the people of Massachusetts.

Then, at Senator Kennedy's suggestion, I went to meet with the Massachusetts Speaker of the House and the President of the State Senate and asked for something they never had done before, to wit: allow me to meet with the Leadership in caucus 1) to discuss new programs that the Advisory Council had proposed and 2) to see how the Party Chairman could help "sell" their programs to the voters of Massachusetts. Finally they agreed. I believe it was the first time in Massachusetts history that a party leader was allowed to sit in on a caucus of the leadership. It also was the first time in memory that the Democratic Party of Massachusetts was a coordinated entity, working together on behalf of the electorate. Unity was the watchword.

I tried to get rank and file Democrats to "join the party" for $10 dollars a year so they could receive a monthly newsletter and membership card I had created. I even tried a $25 family day in the middle of the State where, in addition to hamburgs, hot dogs, sodas, and clowns for the kids, we were able to convince the great Louis Armstrong and his All Stars to give a concert (gratis). Even though only 300 people were there, Mr. Armstrong gave as full a concert as he would have given to 30,000 people. He was wonderful. The only problem was Ted Kennedy who, after the concert went on for more than an hour, was getting "nudgy". He sat beside me in the front row as the crowd went crazy for Mr. Armstrong, cheering him on and demanding encore after encore which graciously were given. But Ted had a major commitment back in Boston and had to leave. He couldn't very well walk out on Louis Armstrong, so he whispered to me to see what I could do to end the concert. So, between songs, I announced that Mr. Armstrong had a performance to give that evening so we had to let him and his musicians go. Then Ted and I high-tailed it out of the picnic grounds and ran across a huge field to the adjoining airport where the Kennedy plane, "The Caroline", was waiting to take us to Boston. This was the last flight of the Caroline which had been John F. Kennedy's campaign plane before the family turned it over to the Smithsonian – and only Ted and I and the pilot were aboard. On August 11, 1967, in response to my thank-you-note, I received a hand-written letter from Louis Armstrong which I treasure. It read: "Dear Mr. Hyman: Your letter to me was enjoyed "no end" when I received it this morning. Man my All Stars and Myself had a Ball Sunday swingin for the folks. And Senator Kennedy was right in there wailing with us. A day I shall never forget---B'lieve me...From Satchmo, Louis Armstrong." I keep that letter on the wall in my office as one of my most treasured gifts.

Things were going swimmingly...until the roof fell in. We were hit with a political explosion that rocked Massachusetts and the nation, smashing the unity we so carefully had built up, and dividing our leadership in bitter recrimination. I refer to the war in Vietnam and the Presidential campaign of 1968.

The liberal wing of the Democratic Party wanted us out of Vietnam as the wrong war in the wrong place at the wrong time. The conservative wing of the Party believed in the "domino theory" and urged the U.S. to throw everything it had at the Communist menace in the Far East. And a third group felt that the new President (LBJ) knew more than any of us about what was happening in Vietnam and that we should support him and his decisions without question. I saw families divided, friendships ended, and civil dialogue turned into ugly confrontation.

As Chairman of the Massachusetts Democratic Party, I was being pulled in all directions. Most of our Party leaders supported LBJ. The liberals supported Gene McCarthy. Then Bob Kennedy entered the race and seemed to be the putative nominee until his untimely death. The distinguished economist John Kenneth Galbraith wrote me a tongue-in-cheek note about my Chairmanship from his home in Gstaad, Switzerland saying about me "it was nice...to realize that a man can survive what may have been the worst job in the free world".

LBJ surprised everyone by announcing that he would not run for re-election. Soon thereafter Martin Luther King was killed and then Bobby Kennedy was murdered. Hubert Humphrey became the Democratic nominee for President in 1968, and he lost to Richard Nixon.

But something fascinating took place at the 1968 Democratic convention that is known to very few people. Let me tell you about it because I was there as a Massachusetts delegate to the convention and saw it all.

The proceedings at the convention hall in Chicago were an unmitigated disaster from a public relations point of view. The pro-Vietnam War and anti-Vietnam war factions clashed often and rudely. Soon the troubles poured out into the streets. The anti-Vietnam war protesters, many of them very young, taunted the Chicago police who, in turn, vastly overreacted. There were beatings and riots. All of this was on national television. Most of the convention delegates were very unhappy with the situation. They did not want to be limited to having to choose between Hubert Humphrey who continued to support Lyndon Johnson's unpopular Vietnam policy and Gene McCarthy who wanted to get out of Vietnam.

Then things started to get interesting. Rumors began to fly that Ted Kennedy should become a candidate and take up his fallen brother's banner. More and more delegates came to me and said they would support Ted if he would agree to be the Democratic presidential candidate. I was skeptical.

Steve Smith (the Kennedy brother-in-law who ran the business and financial side of the Kennedy family's affairs) called a small group of us together in his hotel suite and told us that, even though there appeared to be a ground-swell for Ted, he wanted us to systematically canvass the delegates and get a hard count as to how much *genuine* support there was for Ted's nomination.

The next day we reported back to Steve and, to everyone's amazement, there were more than enough delegates who stated unequivocally that they would vote for Ted Kennedy as the Party's presidential nominee if he would announce his candidacy. Steve then excused himself and went into the bedroom of his suite to call Ted who was in Hyannisport. After a few minutes, Steve came back into the living room and told us that Ted would *not* allow his name to be placed in nomination and that we should disband our activities on his behalf. I couldn't believe my ears because, so long as I knew them, the Kennedys *never* walked away from a good political opportunity…and this surely was one of the best.

So I went back to my room and placed a call to Ted myself. He came on the line, and I asked him why he was turning down the opportunity, which was "real", to become the Democratic nominee for President. Ted's reply made me respect him tremendously. He said: "There are two reasons why I won't run. The first is that the delegates will be giving the nomination to me because of sympathy for Bobby, not because of me. And second, I am not now prepared to be President of the United States." This rationale I could accept. So that ended the matter. Humphrey became the nominee but he lost to Richard Nixon.

I continued talking with Ted Kennedy about his future national plans. Accordingly I did not seek reelection as Party Chairman and instead moved our family to Washington, D.C. where I accepted a partnership in a noted Washington law firm and kept in close touch with Ted regarding his future.

Ted Kennedy, like his brothers, was wonderful with children. Once, shortly after they were married, Ted's wife Vicki hosted a dinner in Boston for a small group of friends. It was Fathers Day, and, with Vicki's permission, I offered a toast to Ted as a truly great father. He was in a happy and expansive mood that evening, and when we asked him how he was getting along with Vicki's young children, he told us how he loved to go swimming in the pool with them. "One time Vicki's daughter came over to me," said Ted, "and asked me: 'Teddy, can you stand on your head in the pool?' (Note that Ted played all the parts in these stories, perfectly imitating the high-pitched voice of a little girl.) "Yes, I can," I said. "Let's see who can do the best hand stand. You go first". "So," continued Ted, "she dove into the pool and did a very good hand-stand under water. When she came up for air, she said: 'Teddy, how did I do?' And I said: 'you got an 8' and she was very pleased. But then she said: 'now it's your turn, Teddy', so I jumped into the pool and did *my* hand-stand. When I came up, I saw that she was crying. I said: 'What's wrong?' and she said: 'Teddy, you got a 10!" That's the Ted Kennedy that few people knew.

One summer, shortly after I had been divorced, my wife and I agreed that, while she was living in Boston with my boys, my daughter Elizabeth would stay with me in Washington for the summer. She was 13 years old at the time. Since I was heavily involved in a legal matter at my law firm, I could spend only weekends but not weekdays with Elizabeth, and I didn't know how to keep her occupied while I was at work. So finally I called my friend Senator Ted Kennedy and told him that I realized that literally hundreds of young people apply for summer jobs in his office, often years in advance, but I wondered whether he could help me place Elizabeth in some kind of job in some other office in the Capitol, maybe in the mail room, to keep her busy at a difficult time for her. Ted didn't miss a beat and said: "Leshta, she comes to work for me tomorrow." That's what I mean about Kennedy loyalty. And so she did…and loved it. One day when I was in my law office, I called the Senator's office and asked to speak with Elizabeth to see how she was doing. The receptionist put me through to my daughter. "Are you having a good time?" I asked. "Oh, yes", she said. "Well, where are you?" "Oh", she said, "I'm here with Senator Kennedy in his office." "Well what you are you doing there?" "We're having chocolate ice cream and brownies together," she said. Until Ted died, he always kept in touch with Elizabeth as she became a beautiful woman and a Washington business leader.

One day when I was Massachusetts Democratic Party Chairman, Ted Kennedy called me and said that he needed to talk with me immediately about some Party issues…but that he had to fly to Hyannis to visit with his father (Ambassador Joseph P. Kennedy) who was quite ill after having suffered a severe stroke… and would I mind flying with him so we could discuss the issues he was concerned about while on the plane. I said "of course". It was a small private plane so it was just the two of us and the pilot. When we arrived at the airport, there was a car waiting to take us to the Ambassador's lovely house in what came to be called "the Kennedy compound". We immediately went into the living room and sat down at a table. Soon Ambassador Kennedy was brought in in a wheelchair. There were just the three of us there. Ted kissed his father on the forehead and then began to talk to him, bringing him the latest political news. The Ambassador could not speak but instead made only terrible guttural sounds as Ted spoke. Soon, as lunch was about to be served, I asked Ted whether I could talk with him privately for a moment. He agreed and we went into the next room. I told him that I felt very awkward being there...that his father didn't know me at all...and surely did not want me, a stranger, to see him in this terrible condition...and could I possibly wait in the next room while Ted talked with his father. At that point, Ted actually teared up, thanked me for my sensitivity, and arranged for me to be served my lunch in an adjoining room. It was a very moving moment. I learned later that, of all the Kennedy children, it was Ted who, no matter how busy he was, regularly came to visit with his father and bring him all the latest political news. That surely spoke very well of Ted.

Like his brothers before him, Ted, in 1968, wrote a book called "Decisions for a Decade". In my opinion, the words he wrote then are equally applicable today. Here's what he wrote: "To some, the condition of modern America is a cause for despair or pessimism. To some, the coming decade appears one of insurmountable problems. I do not believe this is the case. This nation has always met and conquered the threats it has faced – to its survival, to its unity, to its economic security."

"To Lester- Whose energies and talents can help make the decisions easier for all of us. Ted Kennedy, November 1968, Washington, D.C."

Sargent Shriver and Eunice Kennedy Shriver

R. Sargent Shriver Jr., the brother-in-law of John F, Kennedy, was known to one and all as "Sarge"...he was a diplomat, politician and activist. He was the driving force behind the creation of both the Peace Corps and the poverty program and founded the Job Corps and Head Start. He was U.S. Ambassador to France. He also was the Democratic Party's nominee for Vice President in 1972. He was one of the most delightful people I ever have had the privilege of knowing. He was married to Eunice Kennedy, sister of John F. Kennedy, which made him the brother-in-law of JFK. He was utterly charming, full of good humor, and totally enthusiastic about everything that he did. I often have thought that those very enthusiasms prevented him from achieving the highest office in the land for all the wrong reasons. Americans seem to expect that their leaders always to appear to be terribly serious – "gravamen" is the fancy word for it. Many people accused Sarge of being "childlike" -- he wasn't. He was an extremely serious man who thought deeply about issues and displayed consistently good judgment in analyzing policy issues. But he was "childlike" in his enthusiasms – he showed his wonderment as a function of his ebullient intellectual curiosity – and I see nothing wrong with that at all. Quite to the contrary, I think it's just terrific.

One day in the late 60's he called me and asked whether I would like to join him as he campaigned for the Democratic ticket in the mid-western part of the United States. He said that he wanted me to come with him strictly as a friend to keep him company. I was delighted and agreed immediately. We had a grand time on the road and Sarge maintained his high spirits throughout. In Minnesota one cold evening he bellied up to the bar in a blue collar neighborhood and blithely asked for a Courvoisier. The bartender said that he hadn't heard about that kind of beer.

Then he told an audience how delighted he was to be in St. Cloud (but he pronounced it the French way: "San Clew") and the Mayor had to inform him of the correct way to pronounce it (Saint Cloud).

In Michigan he was invited by his hosts to go water-skiing on the lake where we were visiting. Sarge never ducked a challenge, so he borrowed a bathing suit and off he went. All the office-holders and their wives lined up on the porch of the house where we were staying watching Ambassador Shriver's athletic grace and skill. Unfortunately, however, the bathing suit he had borrowed was too big, and in the middle of the lake, it fell considerably. Sarge just grinned, yanked it up, and kept right on going.

When we were campaigning in Montana, Sarge was invited to see a copper mine. He agreed. He asked me and another friend of his, the author Michael Novak, whether we'd like to join him. We said "yes".

However, when we got to the mine, someone asked whether we would like to take an elevator down thousands of feet *into* the mine. I was petrified, having heard horrible stories about mine explosions. But Sarge, always delighted to try something new, said "yes, I'd love to go" and asked if he could bring his two friends along with him. Both Michael Novak and I tried to talk our way out of it, but Sarge would have none of it. An elevator took us what seemed like forever down into the mine where a photo was taken of the three of us. Later Sarge sent it to me along with his hand-written inscription which said: "To: Les Hyman - Your light is brighter than mine, but the sign reveals the important truth that Novak & U are the mine stretchers! And for clinchers, just compare those waist lines. /s/ Sarge."

In South Dakota we had an Advance Man named Michael Goodman who drove us crazy insisting that we always be precisely on schedule at a time when Sarge liked to improvise depending upon the situation. One morning Sarge told me in glee how we could get even with Michael. We went to a local fire station where somehow Sarge convinced the firemen to loan him their fire-truck for a few minutes. He climbed into the driver's seat, and I manned the firebell. We drove past our hotel where our advance man, Michael, was standing out in front fuming because we weren't there on time according to our schedule. Just as we neared him, Sarge turned on the siren, I began to ring the firebell and, when Michael looked up, he saw us waving to him as we sped by. He became apoplectic until he caught on to the joke and laughed along with us.

It was not easy for Sargent Shriver to be a member of the Kennedy family because, as an in-law, he always was reminded that he was not a "genuine" Kennedy. As our little plane flew into a mid-Western airport for a campaign stop, Sarge was reading the local newspaper and blurted out to me in frustration: "I don't mind being described as Sargent Shriver, the brother-in-law of President Kennedy...in fact I'm pretty proud of that. I don't even mind being described as Sargent Shriver, the brother-in-law of Robert Kennedy. But the local paper here doesn't even use my name at all but only says here in a headline that "Brother-in-law of Edward M. Kennedy (who was at least 15 years younger than Sarge) visits our city today". That hurt, said Sarge.

We had many good talks long into the night. Sarge and I spoke often of the civil rights movement in our country. He told me how appalled he was when, in Mississippi, he had managed to raise funds to build a supermarket for the folks in the poorest part of that city...but, within days of the dedication ceremony, the citizens there burned it down. He found this incomprehensible until he asked the people why such a thing could happen. "Because", they replied, "no one asked *us* what kind of facility we wanted." He learned then that one must never condescend to people by giving them what *you* think *they* need—instead you must consult with them and make sure that what is provided by government is something *they* really want and need.

He very movingly described the Head Start program and recalled being in a classroom of black pre-school children in the South when a white State policeman came in to talk with them...and how their initial reaction (understandably) was one of fear...but how, with time and patience, they came to realize that the police could help them, not just hurt them.

In Wisconsin we shared adjoining bedrooms in a motel suite, and at 4 in the morning when I was trying to get some sleep, I heard the telephone ringing. When it stopped, I turned over and went back to sleep. In the morning I asked Sarge who in his right mind would be calling at that ungodly hour. He said that it was his wife, Eunice Kennedy Shriver, calling from their home in Maryland. I asked whether anything was wrong. "No," he said, "everything's fine; she just wanted to know how I was doing on the trip. But I did ask Euni why on earth she would call me at such an ungodly hour, and her reply was 'Not here'! (pronounced as "not heah" in Kennedy-speak). "That's a Kennedy for you," said Sarge.

I once asked Sarge to describe Eunice for me. He said: "John F, Kennedy". I said: "What do you mean?" He replied that she had the same bone structure, the same speaking voice, and the same ironic sense of humor. Later I really got to know Eunice and found his description to be quite accurate. She was extremely bright, and we had some spirited discussions about the many wars that were fought in the name of religion. She also said that if I could find a nice Catholic girl for one of her boys, she would find a nice Jewish boy for my daughter. Eunice made Special Olympics a truly great organization and raised millions of dollars for that wonderful cause. She loved to play sports and once inveigled me to join one of the famous Kennedy touch football games in the Shriver's back yard. I confess that I'm a pretty poor athlete but I tried. Eunie (as Sarge called her) was on the opposite side from mine and when a pass was thrown to her, I jumped up and slapped it down. "You cahnt do that", she said. "But that's what I'm *supposed* to do when I play defense," I said. Next time, when I was trying to catch a pass, she tackled me so hard that I had a backache for days. Like all the Kennedys, she played for keeps. One day I was at an affair at the John F Kennedy library. Hundreds of people were there in black tie and lovely gowns. Eunice came looking for me and said: "Let's get out of here and I'll show you something special". We left the main room and headed for another small room where a projector was set up to show just the two of us the film of President Kennedy's wedding to Jacqueline Bouvier. Eunice narrated the whole thing for me. It was like she was re-living this rare and glorious day in the life of the Kennedy family. It was a marvelous moment. She was a great lady.

Snapshot

John F. Kennedy, Jr.

When John was a student at Brown University (my alma mater), he spent a summer vacation as an intern for the Washington "think tank" The Center for National Policy...I was, and still am, a Board member of that organization (now called The Truman Center for National Policy). One day John told me that he was interested in the theater, so I asked him if he would like to see an off-Broadway musical here in Washington. He said that he would like very much to do that because he loved the theater, so one evening we went there together with my friend Brien McCarthy, a Catholic priest. A few days later John and I had lunch together with my daughter Elizabeth who then was a slightly pudgy teen-ager and who, forever more, has chastised me that I should have taken her to meet John as the beautiful grown-up woman that she now is. At any rate, soon after the luncheon get-together with John, he told me that his real ambition was to be in the theater but that he couldn't consider it. "Why not?" I asked. "Because", he replied, "I would be given parts not because I'm such a great actor but because I'm the son of John F. Kennedy...and that wouldn't be fair." "On the other hand," he said, "if I adopted a stage name, I would be disrespecting my father's memory". I was impressed by his analysis.

On another occasion, John called me and suggested that I read a certain novel by William Kennedy (no relation)...I did so, and when I got back to him to tell him how much I enjoyed the book, I asked him how he reacted to a certain chapter. "Oh. I never read the book myself", said John. "Then why," I responded, "did you recommend to *me* a book that *you* haven't even read?" "Because", he said, "my mother read it and she has impeccable taste and she thought the book was terrific". John really idolized his mother.

Many years later when I had lost touch with John who then was living in New York, I was at the prestigious Gridiron Club dinner in Washington (where we all had to wear white tie and tails!) and I noticed that John was at a nearby table. I was astounded when he got up, came over to my table and said: "Les, how are you?" It made my day that he remembered, proving that he would have been a great politician... perhaps one day even President of the United States. John's death was a mortal blow to the entire Kennedy family which has suffered so many deaths over the years.

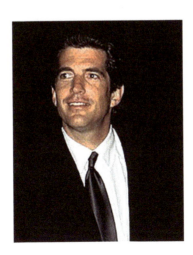

It should be noted that, although John and Bob and Ted no longer are with us, generations of Kennedys continue to carry the torch. Just a few examples are:

Vicki Kennedy (widow of EMK) is President of the Board of the Edward M. Kennedy Library;

Kathleen Kennedy Townsend (eldest daughter of RFK) was Lt. Governor of Maryland;

Patrick Kennedy (son of EMK) is a mental health advocate;

Joseph Kennedy III (son of former Congressman Joe Kennedy II) is a Member of Congress;

Caroline Kennedy (JFK's daughter) was U.S. Ambassador to Japan;

Ted Kennedy Jr. (EMK's son) is a State Senator in Connecticut;

Kerry Kennedy (daughter of RFK) is a human rights activist;

Rory Kennedy (daughter of RFK) is a documentary film maker;

Robert F. Kennedy Jr. (son of RFK) is an environmental attorney;

And there are so many more.

About the Author

LESTER S. HYMAN, LAWYER AND STRATEGIC ADVISOR

Lester S. Hyman is a Washington, D.C. attorney with more than 60 years of experience in law, business, politics, the arts and international affairs.

After serving in the federal government as an attorney with the U.S. Securities and Exchange Commission and later as Senior Consultant to the Secretary of U.S. Housing and Urban Development, Mr. Hyman returned to his home state of Massachusetts where, as a protege of John F. Kennedy, he was Chief Assistant to the Governor, Secretary of Commerce and Development, and Chairman of the Democratic Party of that State. He also has taught at the Kennedy School of Government at Harvard University.

He then returned to Washington where he was a founder of the prominent law firm of Swidler Berlin representing major business clients both in the United States: (20th Century Fox, McGraw Hill) and overseas: France (Roussel-Uclaf), Germany (Hoechst), Japan (Matsushita, Mazda), Korea (Hyundai), as well as representing a number of countries (Haiti, Liberia, Bermuda, and the Virgin Islands).

Mr. Hyman has been very active in international peace resolution work in Africa and Central America where he has worked closely with former President Jimmy Carter and the International Negotiating Network. He was President Clinton's representative at the signing of the Guatemala Peace Treaty as well as Clinton's appointee to the Franklin D. Roosevelt Memorial Commission. He is the author of the 2003 book "U.S. Policy Towards Liberia".

He currently serves on the Boards of the Truman Center for National Policy, the Center for Advanced Defense Studies (C4ADS), and the International Intellectual Property Institute (IIPI).

As a devotee of the arts, Mr. Hyman served on the D.C. Arts and Humanities Council, and the Boards of the Norton Simon Museum of Art and the Dana Tai Soon Burgess Dance Company. In education, he was a member of the Board of the University of the District of Columbia and for 30 years served on the Board of the H. Lavity Stoutt Community College in the British Virgin Islands.

CPSIA information can be obtained
at www.ICGtesting.com
Printed in the USA
BVHW092009110219
540023BV00001B/2/P